A Passion for Puffins

Natural History books
by W R Mitchell

A FEW MILLION BIRDS
WILD PENNINES
BIRDWATCH AROUND SCOTLAND
WILD CUMBRIA
PENNINE BIRDS (with Bill Robson)
LAKELAND BIRDS (with Bill Robson)
LAKELAND MAMMALS (with Peter Delap)
BIRD WATCHING IN YORKSHIRE (with R F Dickens)
A YEAR WITH THE CURLEWS
HIGHLAND SPRING
WEST HIGHLAND SUMMER
HIGHLAND AUTUMN
HIGHLAND WINTER
ST. KILDA: A VOYAGE TO THE EDGE OF THE WORLD

A Passion for Puffins

by W R Mitchell
Illustrated in line and colour by David Binns

CASTLEBERG
1994

for JEAN AND KURT REINSCH

Muckle Flugga
and Outrock

Hermaness

Noss

Shiant Is.

Westray

Clo Mor

Flannan Is.

St Kilda

Berneray and
Mingulay

Treshnish Is.

Farne Is.

Bempton and
Flamborough

Published by Castleberg, 18 Yealand Avenue, Giggleswick,
Settle, North Yorkshire, BD24 0AY

Typeset in Clearface and printed by Lamberts Printers,
Station Road, Settle, North Yorkshire, BD24 9AA

ISBN: 1 871064 92 9

Contents

Puffins Galore	7
The Puffins Return	17
Flamborough:	
Yorkshire's 'Little Denmark'	19
Farne Islands:	
Saints and Seabirds	26
Life in the Burrow	33
Treshnish Islands:	
A Seat Among the Puffins	35
Mingulay:	
Wild Water off the Hebrides	41
Cape Wrath:	
A Place for Turning	57
Orkney:	
Low Green Isles	62
Shetland:	
Land of the Simmer Dim	66
St Kilda:	
By Gemini to Dun	81
The Fledglings Depart	86
Iceland:	
Land of Fire and Water	87
Reykjavik:	
Shopping for Puffins	95
Westman Islands:	
By Air to Heimaey	102
Northern Iceland:	
Fast Boat to Puffin Island	106
Grimsey:	
A Speck in the Ocean	111

The Atlantic Puffin

Fratercula arctica
(also known as Lundi, Sea-parrot, Tammy Norrie, Pilot,
Coulter and Bougir)

...a fat and consequential little bird. (George Seaton, 1876).

...like a respectable butler at his master's door, in a black coat and white waistcoat, with a Roman nose red at the tip with many a bottle of port. (*North British Review,* May, 1864).

Puffins...looking solemn and important with their bibulous noses, grey cheeks, black coats and white waistcoats. (F Fraser Darling, on North Rona, 1938).

The puffin...can look very wise as it sits on the cliff-edge, apparently speculating on the meaning of life. (Hjalmar R Bardarson, 1986).

The great parrot-bill is enlarged by bands of bright decoration, while a false triangular eyebrow over a red-trimmed eye on a whitened face gives it an air of earnest bewilderment. (Colin Harrison, 1988).

...bright fantastic dolls—but alive! (Robert Atkinson, 1949).

Their feet are bright orange and when shuffling from their holes, the puffins resemble old men in bright orange carpet slippers. (Thomas M Goring, watching puffins at Bass Rock).

Puffins Galore...

MY first puffin looked like a bumble bee against the sea-glare. A small, rotund body was supported by short wings which operated so quickly they were just a blur. I fancied that if they had stopped beating for an instant, the puffin would have dropped from the sky.

I had previously seen the puffin only on the printed page, where it looked large and imposing, like a penguin. Even then, I recognised the puffin as something special. It stared at me with a red-rimmed eye. The triangular beak—tinted red, yellow and blue—was fantastic: like a false nose donned by a clown.

In contrast, the puffin which zoomed in from the sea for a landfall on the chalk cliffs of Flamborough was a midget.

That day I followed a cliff-edge footpath from North Landing, where a blue-ganseyed fisherman said the local name for the bird was 'Pilot'. He added: 'Don't ask me why it was called Pilot. It nests in holes among rocks. I once put my hand into a hole, looking for an egg. All I got for my pains was a nip from its neb (beak). And what a nip! It made my eyes water...'

7

My puffin vigil seemed to last half a lifetime. I stared seawards, and along the cliffs, until my eyes prickled with fatigue. Then, idly scanning the silvered sea, I saw my first live puffin whir into view and settle on a ledge. It was a puffin, sure enough—but disappointingly small. The bird cocked its head to return my stare.

On that spring day, almost fifty years ago, I became 'puffin daft'. The Yorkshire coast was warm and windless. The clarity was such, and the tones so bright, I might have been watching a sequence from a travel film.

At North Landing, the clinker-built fishing boats, known as cobles, lay on the beach like multi-coloured sea creatures which had hauled themselves from the water to sunbathe. Questioned about puffins, that old fisherman said: 'We had a stuffed puffin in a glass case till my mother got fed up of dusting it.'

A cobalt-blue sea contrasted with the white cliffs. These were overtopped by clay and thatched with grass and a profusion of wild flowers. The bird-busy sky was a cornflower blue.

Puffins do not live in a vacuum. Along the cliffs was a tumult of nesting seabirds: a blizzard of kittiwakes, each bird forever calling its name, razorbills, standing about like dandies in evening suits, and rows of growling guillemots, like two-tone skittles.

A lazy tide smacked its lips against the cliffs and ran into the many caves; it licked the chalk pebbles on the beach until they gleamed as though from some inner light source. This coast is exposed to a northerly wind: I recalled when the short, sharp sea had boomed against the chalk cliffs and the lazy wind—'it goes right through you, rather than taking t'trouble to go round'—made the telegraph wires shriek.

I lay on the cliff edge, scanning the sea, watching the auks, including the amazing puffin. A newly-arrived bird did not so much alight as plummet, abruptly stopping its wings and dropping with a splash.

Flamborough was not the place to study puffins. Here they do not disport themselves across acres of a cliff top, which has been honeycombed by their nesting burrows—the typical puffin location. Yorkshire puffins are spread thinly and mostly nest in crannies. With the cliffs several hundred feet high, puffin-watching is not for those of a nervous disposition.

My regard for the puffin led me northwards, in easy stages, across waters where Atlantic grey seals showed their heads and stared at me with large, soulful eyes; where razorbills and guillemots scuttered away when disturbed and where gannets, the 'white birds of the herring', were diving, a plume of water marking the point at which a bird entered the sea.

In due course, on the island of Grimsey, I crossed the Arctic Circle under the gaze of dozens of pouting puffins of a northern sub-species.

It was at St Abbs, in south-east Scotland, that I photographed my first puffin. The bird stood on a grassy slope a hundred feet or so above the sea. Having become totally absorbed in my quest for a picture, and moving from one ledge to another, I then had to extricate myself from a precarious position. The puffin watched me, unblinkingly.

On the Treshnish Islands, in western Scotland, I sat down—only to have one of my boots pecked by a puffin. I was covering its burrow. That afternoon, only a small percentage of the total number of puffins was on parade, whereas on Dun, one of the St Kilda group, 'at the edge of the world', puffins formed a living wheel, their flight taking them above sea and land. Village Bay was speckled with puffins.

Everywhere, and always, the feature that first impressed me was that extraordinary triangular beak, which looks large and heavy in profile and yet is astonishingly thin when viewed head-on.

At Noss, in Shetland, I played hide and seek with a puffin. I had the cover of a drystone wall. The bird, a few feet away, had its attention divided. It must also keep an eye on the predatory great black-backed gull, which has a noxious habit, having killed a puffin, of turning the skin inside out so as to pick the bones of its victim.

At Hermaness, within sight of Muckle Flugga, in the far north of Britain, puffins with beaks stuffed with small fish cocked their heads to look at me from a range of a few feet before darting underground to feed their chicks.

Puffin-fever led me to Iceland, which has the largest concentration of Atlantic puffins. When visiting Heimaey, the principal island of the Westman group, I stroked a (stuffed) puffin. It was a bus driver's mascot. He had parked his bus at the edge of a still-warm volcano and was amused by my request to borrow his mascot. It was my turn to be amused when he pointed to the large fishing town and remarked: 'We catch fish. We eat fish. We look like fish!'

At Grimsey, which I visited in the company of an American couple and a Welsh opera singer, I had to run the gauntlet of Arctic terns to come within viewing range of the Arctic form of our puffin which stood on a range of rocks, close to the sea.

Where was the genesis of the remarkable auk family, which is so much at home in the sea it also uses its wings as flippers to produce forward thrust in the green depths of the ocean? Fossils found in rocks laid down some sixty million years ago indicate that puffins were first known in the Pacific. It is theorised that a mere five million years ago, when the Bering Strait was open, the ancestor of our puffin entered the Atlantic. The population is now estimated at fifteen million.

The puffin has what to us are grand situations for its nesting activity—grassy areas on an island or peninsula. Puffins inhabit the stacks and cliffs of the Faeroe Islands.

A friend on a cruise boat which lay near the rock walls of
Flugoya, an island off the Lynggen peninsula of northern Norway,
recalls their dark grandeur and the sight of six white-tailed sea
eagles—'flying barn doors'—which were hunting down puffins for
food. Several exciting pursuits near sea level were noted.

To islanders, through the ages, the presence of seabird colonies,
for several months in the year, represented a feast of eggs or flesh.
The bones of puffins have been found in the middens of early
peoples, such as those inhabiting Jarlshof in Shetland, not far
from Sumburgh Head, where puffins are still breeding.

An Icelandic housewife, who told me how to cook a puffin, was obtaining her supply from a supermarket in Reykjavik. She assured me that the flesh does not have a strong fish flavour.

Islanders are characters—individuals, with their own ideas and points of view. My travels took me to a Hebridean island where a doctor kept me on the doorstep and listened somewhat testily to my description of a stomach disorder. His prescription was: 'F-r-r-resh air, laddie'.

On St Kilda, as the guest of the Army, I patronised the celebrated *Puff Inn,* the local 'watering hole'. The St Kildans lived mainly on the teeming colonies of seabirds, eating puffins and fulmars, fresh in summer and dried in winter. It was on Hirta, the principal island, that I heard of food for the garrison being dropped from an aircraft. When a bag burst, a soldier in the reception group had his shoulder-bone broken—by a frozen chicken.

I read the accounts left by Victorian naturalists who visited 'Puffindom'. They were inclined to write exaggerated reports, though in the west at least they may have had a case. The puffin population has been declining. A fisherman who knew Ailsa Craig stretched the credibility of a visitor in 1888 when he described the swarms of puffins: 'They come twelve raik a day and 156 million thousand at a raik.'

The return of the puffin—this podgy seabird with the colourful neb—marks for me the start of a summer carnival at the coast. The bird must first overcome its timidity on returning to *terra firma* after about seven months at sea. It does so with crowds of puffins around, for comfort, support and as a ploy to confuse attacking gulls and skuas.

The puffin does not seem to mind being stared at from a range of a few yards, though it conceals much of its nesting activity in a burrow. The bird is notable for that multi-coloured beak and the big hazel eyes with their red orbital rings.

Nothing much seems to happen during the day, unless birds are arriving with food for the young. It is towards night, against an orange-red afterglow, that an air display is to be seen—a host of puffins, flying in shape of a huge wheel. The numbers in the wheel may appear constant, yet it is being joined by new birds while others are descending to their nesting places.

The puffin, a loner in winter, enjoys being one of a crowd in the nesting season, while maintaining the territorial integrity of its nesting burrow with dramatic displays which, if not heeded by the intruder, lead to a fight. In a 'puffinry', it is safest for a bird to be in the midst of things. The pufling in its burrow grows up with the noise and bustle of a colony all around it.

The hub-bub and the undertone of puffin growling impressed those Victorian writers who wrote—with passion—of 'countless thousands' of puffins seen at their historic island haunts, such as the Shiants off Lewis.

A visitor in 1888 noted, with excitement: 'The sea, the sky and the land seemed populated by equal proportions, each vast in itself—a constantly moving, whirling, eddying, seething throng of life, drifting and swooping and swinging in the wind, or pitching and heaving on the water, or crowding and jostling on the ledges and rocks... or perched like small white specks far up in the cliff-face amongst the giant basalt columns.'

Many writers have compared the puffin's 'dress suit' of black and white, its upright stance and rolling walk with, say, a fussy little alderman at a civic reception. Seeing a group of gossiping puffins at a cliff edge, it is hard not to make comparisons with humankind. (A crowd of jabbering bankers at an annual dinner brings to my mind a penguin rookery).

The puffin looks cuddly but is not cuddlesome, except in its soft-toy form. In real life, this bird is one of nature's 'toughies', able to fend for itself.

The range is impressive—from Eastern Egg Rock, in the United States, to the Kola peninsula, by the Barents Sea; and from Haklyt Island, in north-west Greenland, to Ushant, off the coast of Brittany, taking in the teeming colonies of Newfoundland, Iceland and northern Britain.

Three sub-species have been described—*F.a.grabae* (the Faeroes, Southern Norway, Britain and France), *F.a. arctica* (Newfoundland to Scandinavia, taking in part of Greenland and Iceland) and the almost mythical *F.a. naumanni,* denizen of Greenland and Spitzbergen, the furthermost north of Puffindom).

The puffin is suited to its chilly habitat, having the thermal insulation of thick down next to the skin and a tight and oily plumage. That large beak, striped with pale blue, yellow and glowing red, is not just a decorative touch. This is a status symbol, proclaiming seniority. With its horny patches, grown for the nesting season and then jettisoned at the onset of winter, a puffin's neb changes in size and appearance with each succeeding year. A slim, unridged bill indicates that the wearer is less than two years of age. A single ridge on the bill marks out a bird of between two and three years old. Two ridges are associated with the mature puffin.

To a small bird which burns up energy fast, the bill is adapted for holding fish, a dozen or so at a time, thus sparing an intense shuttle service with supplies when the parents are tending a chick. One load of sand eels or other small fish will assuage the chick's hunger for a while. Used as a weapon, the beak of a puffin has the cutting power of a pair of secateurs.

I am amused by the small patches of blue feathers, forming 'eyebrows', for they give the puffin a droll appearance. At times it looks bewildered. Because a puffin is 'cute', it has become a prime subject for decorating tea-towels. The puffin stares at us from the dust-jackets of innumerable books. In reality, this dumpy auk stands less than a foot high and has a serious attitude towards a

life in which only the most resourceful survive.

The wings double-up as flippers, generating brisk forward movement when the bird seeks fish-food in the green marine world. Being relatively small, the wings are flapped at a frantic speed— from three hundred to four hundred beats a minute when the bird is airborne. The flight feathers are moulted during the early months of the year, just before the puffin's return to land. The flightless puffin has to ride out the Atlantic storms. The orange feet are webbed, acting as air-brakes when the puffin is in flight and as rudders when submerged.

The puffin has an uneasy manner, forever looking over its shoulder, as well it might, having many enemies. The Arctic skua 'locks on' to a fish-carrying puffin like a missile, harassing the luckless bird until it drops the fish, which the skua sweeps up in mid-air.

The nesting areas, enriched by bird droppings, have a profusion of spring flowers—sea pink, white campion and bluebell. They form a colourful setting for the gregarious, ever-curious puffin, which takes short walks, as though to check up on the neighbours and will investigate any strange object, including a snare set by a fowler.

Puffins have not a great deal to say and may occasionally utter a conversational *aah*—something of a growl. Actions speak louder than words. A puffin communicates by its posture and by use of that huge painted beak.

Two birds, facing each other, clatter their large flattish beaks together. Bizarre posturing conveys its feelings. A puffin walks in a slow, exaggerated way, keeping its body as straight as a ramrod, puffing out its breast and resting its beak against it. Simultaneously, it flirts its small tail.

Bird-watchers with breathing equipment follow the puffin into the sea and watch it pursuing its fish prey underwater. Air bubbles, lodged in the bird's plumage, give it a silvery sheen as it propels itself with its wings, using its webbed feet for steering. Any excess salt taken in while fishing is disposed of through special nasal glands.

Its nesting activity is hidden from us in a burrow driven into peaty ground. The newly-fledged puffin usually chooses a dark night to leave the nursery. It scuttles to the sea and paddles into the unknown, not to return to its natal area for a year or two.

Puffins disperse, going far out to sea. They spend the winter—who knows where?

Young puffins.

16

The Puffins Return...

IN THE early spring, on rocky parts of the coast where tides merge and mix, the sea blooms. Minute forms of plant life, the phytoplankton, are energised by the sun and nurtured by nutrients in the upper layers of the sea, where tropical water mixes with cold currents from the Arctic.

The plant material is food for zooplankton, and so on up the food chain to the fish which sustain the seabirds.

Millions of birds converge to nest where the food is most abundant. Puffins frequent the chalk walls of Flamborough, the dolerite stacks of the Farnes, the cliffscapes near Cape Wrath, Noss, Hermaness, and a string of islands which are like stepping stones in the cold Atlantic. Lengthening days trigger off the impulse to breed. The puffins, which in winter are widespread across the ocean, now turn towards the areas where they were reared.

The wintering puffin is drab. With the moult, it is transformed. The grey of the mantle becomes a shiny black and the dull-looking underparts whiten. The beak, which in the off-season is slim and greyish-yellow, acquires blue horny patches and the bright nuptial colours, plus a yellow wattle at the base.

The puffin is back within sight of land. The sea is speckled with birds, which are nervous, easily disturbed, flying out to sea for a few days and then returning, bee-like in their numbers and appearance, their rotund bodies upheld by whirring wings.

With such a throng, the puffins keep in contact with shoals of fish—their main source of food. The female puffins in particular must dine well to bring themselves into a good condition for egg-laying and incubation.

Gradually, the emphasis shifts from a sea-going life to one that is divided between sea and land. Each mature puffin is drawn not just to the tract of cliff-top on which it nested last year but, in most cases, to the precise burrow.

There is safety in numbers. A few birds pitch down warily on land. The rest soon follow. If the wind is tricky, a puffin may go head-over-heels on the spongy turf, taking the knocks without injury because of its skeletal toughness and lagging of down and feathers.

Many of the puffins are paired. They rub beaks. Out at sea, they copulate, with the males standing—balancing with their beating wings—on the backs of the partly submerged females. On land, the pair bond is reinforced by a nibbling of head and neck. A male gallantly presents the female with a token—a feather or a tuft of grass.

Among younger birds, competition is keen for the best sites. In territorial disputes, the offended puffin faces the intruder with its beak held low: a sign of defiance, not of submission. The warning is usually strong enough to deter the stranger.

Not all the puffins have come back. Numerous young birds delay their return until summer, when they will come ashore, prospecting for nesting sites. By then, the old birds will be caring for well-developed young. . .

Flamborough:
Yorkshire's 'Little Denmark'

LENGTHENING days bring the seabirds to their nesting sites on the cliffs of Yorkshire's east coast. Dove-grey kittiwakes, powerfully winged fulmars, quaint little auks—the puffins—after travelling thousands of miles over open seas, cease their oceanic wanderings and head for the white cliffs.

Other seabirds, less venturesome, which winter off shore or over coastal waters also wing towards land. These are the dark brown and white guillemots and the black and white razorbills.

A sunny day of calm seas attracts birds to the cliffs. With the advent of rough weather, they return to sea. Gradually towards April their visits become more frequent and of longer duration. In May, nesting begins in earnest.

A Norman Handley, 1949.

THE TALL cliffs of the headland, which were like those of their own country, lured savage Viking warriors here. Outstanding columns of rock were named by them.

One small bay they dedicated to the god Thor, and it is still known as Thornwick Bay. And another bay, where seals once disported, was named Selsick, or the bay of seals.

The most interesting, however, is Stottle Bink. 'Stothul' signifies a station and 'Bink' a shelf. Near the summit of this high cliff is a ledge on which a 'look-out' stood to watch for enemy craft. Even today, the place where the fishermen stow their fishing-gear they call the 'bink'.

George Hardwick, 1944.

JUST north of Bridlington, flinty chalk, meagre in fossils, is capped by boulder clay and thatched by sweet-scented grasses and wild flowers. The chalk extends eastward as the white cliffs of Flamborough, Bempton and Speeton.

Old folk call this area 'Little Denmark', after the Scandinavian settlers of the Viking age. The Constable family, who owned much land, paid a token rent to the King of Denmark each year by firing an arrow bearing a gold coin from the headland into the sea.

When I first travelled to Flamborough, attracted by the teeming seabird life, I used a rickety car, taking three hours to cross Yorkshire, motoring against the grain of the landscape. I felt a mounting excitement at what I would see—a village roofed by red pantiles, swept by salt breezes; cliffs, hundreds of feet high, and North Landing, a recess in those cliffs, where cobles, the in-shore fishing boats of the North East coast, were launched from a sandy beach.

On a sunny day, it was hurtful to look at the gleaming cliffs and the sea-glare. Sometimes, I cadged a lift on a boat and, as it bobbed off the white walls of Flamborough or Bempton, I watched seabirds—guillemots, smooth as cigars; razorbills, which are dandies, clad in immaculate black-and-white with beaks reminiscent of the old-fashioned 'cut throat'.

Kittiwakes were forever shouting their names and turning each indentation of the cliff into an echo-chamber and, of course, there were pouting puffins, the Flamborough Pilots.

Richard Cowling, who had been a fisherman for thirty years when I first met him, told me of the constrictions of North Landing. 'A man has to be brought up to the place to be comfortable in it. The worst sea we can have is from the north, and it happens to be a north-easter—it comes straight in!'

Mr and Mrs Tant Cross told me about local folklore.

Not even the Norse folk, worshippers of Thor and Odin, could have been more superstitious than the folk of Flamborough. Wool was never wound by lamplight nor would anyone from Flamborough go outside with a lighted candle (yet one might light the candle out of doors).

No one had to walk over the fishing lines, and no one must mention 'pig' at the Landing. A parson in a silk hat was a symbol of bad luck. A fisherman who saw one would promptly say: 'Oh, laws, drum's up—we sall ev nwea mare good luck this week.'

I had many of Tant's stories in mind as I explored this part of the Yorkshire coast, where in the early morning light the cliffs gleam like icebergs. The summer sun rises and sets over water, leaving the bird-cliffs in shadow during the day.

At other times, a sea-fret, known as a roke, drapes the cliffs like a wet dish-clout. Gusts of wind in excess of a hundred miles an hour have been recorded on the cliff-tops. As a former coastguard said: 'At Flamborough, there's always a breeze of some sort.'

Fifty thousand pairs of birds nest on these cliffs. An eighteenth century visitor, Thomas Pennant, wrote of 'innumerable flocks which quite cover the face of the cliffs' and of multitudes which 'swarmed in the air and almost stunned us with the variety of their croaks and screams.'

The puffin appears at the breeding cliffs in April, by which time the other auks are well-established. I would sit between tufts of sea pinks and idly scan the sea through binoculars, picking out the first of the returning puffins.

When I first ventured into these parts, my bible was Nelson's *Birds of Yorkshire.* I read that pure white puffins had been seen on the cliffs. The lack of pigment must have rendered them virtually invisible against the chalk.

The vast scale of the Bempton cliffs is unexpected, for at popular Bridlington, to the south, the cliffscape has given way to a low shoreline. Long before a present bird reserve was established, with its interpretation centre and car park, I left my car beside a ditch at the end of the cul de sac road and followed the fieldside to the cliff edge.

One moment, I was in a landscape holding a springtime flush of green grass, with corn buntings calling, and the next moment I was looking down on a blizzard of kittiwakes, unprepared for the tumultuous chorus in which every bird contributed its *kitti-waake, kitti-waake* to the general din.

Puffin-watching on the chalk cliffs is not easy. The birds are well-scattered and there seems to be no special pattern to their comings and goings—at least until the young have hatched and the parents operate a shuttle-service with food.

I found it difficult to distinguish between breeding and non-breeding birds. All appeared to enjoy their spells of hanging about the cliff edges. I detected that conversational *aah*—something of a growl. Two birds, facing each other, reinforced the pair bond by clattering each other's beaks.

It amused me to see a puffin lean forward at the entrance to its nesting burrow and peer into the hole for minutes on end, as though expecting something to pop out.

At Bempton, I met the local gang of four 'cliff-climmers', named after their climbing accomplishments, evolved over some two hundred and fifty years with the object of collecting seabird eggs. The 'climmer' wore old clothes, had a metal helmet on his head and studded boots on his feet, so that he might have a good grip against the slippery ledges.

Wearing a special harness, he was lowered off the cliff on a three hundred foot long hempen rope, the other end being attached to an iron stake driven firmly into the ground. He sought the pear-shaped guillemot eggs, which had been laid on open ledges. At flush time, between three hundred and four hundred eggs were collected in a single descent, being placed in canvas sacks.

The most attractively marked eggs went to collectors; the rest were for human consumption. One of the climmers told me: 'There's nowt to t'job—providing you don't look down.'

I was shown a directory for 1831 which mentioned that during the incubation period, boys collected bushels of eggs for the sugar house in Hull and for domestic reasons. 'In the summertime, many generations come hither from Bridlington, Scarborough and other places to enjoy the sport of shooting, and so clouded is the air with feathered tribes that the worst marksman may kill in a short time more than he can carry.'

Ralph Chislett, who laboured hard and long to protect the bird life of Yorkshire, referred to the Bempton 'egg racket'. When the Bempton 'climmers' told him that the richly-marked eggs, fetching a special price in former days, are rarely seen now, he pointed out the obvious reason: that the few individual birds producing such eggs had not survived. The 'climmers' knew the corners on the cliffs at which to find them.

Puffin eggs were costly to the 'climmers' in the sense they were difficult to gather, resting at the end of burrows or among the rocks. If the puffin was still in its nesting hole when the climmer reached it, he offered the bird a beakful of grass. While the bird's attention was claimed by the grass, the man took the egg.

No longer are the puffins of Flamborough culled, as they are in Iceland, Faeroes and Norway, though not to excess. At some celebrated Norwegian puffinries, special hounds were bred to catch young birds as they left the colony at night. These dogs were relatively small, nimble and with feet evolved to give a good grip on the rocks. They did not bark and any young puffins they collected were brought back to the fowler uninjured.

In Iceland and the Faeroes, it is mainly non-breeders that fall to the *fleyg,* a triangular net with wooden supports which is lashed to a long pole. The Faeroese use decoy birds to appeal to the puffin's natural curiosity. Traditionally, when eaten, puffin was stuffed with a cake mixture and roasted. Boiled puffin was preferred in Norway and Icelanders were partial to smoked puffin. On St Kilda, puffin was dried for use in winter, when several were put in the cooking pot. If puffin was eaten shortly after being caught, it was usually roasted before the peat fire—an ignoble end.

Guillemots and a pear-shaped egg.

Farne Islands:
Saints and Seabirds

ON FOUR visits to Seahouses, the North Sea was a tumult of water and spray as easterly gales froliced through the region. Water slopped over the harbour wall. Keel boots in the recesses of the harbour tugged and fidgetted at their moorings.

Viewed from the Northumberland shore, the Farnes resembled a flotilla of lean warships, pewter-grey in the half light, with water creaming at their bows. An old fisherman—there's always an old fisherman handy in such places as Seahouses—illustrated a talent for under-statement when he said: 'It's a bit of a blow.'

Even when the waves are not breaking or capped by white spume, the North Sea can be daunting to a landlubber. A swell might be nothing more than an unpleasant undulation of ridges and troughs. Or those ridges can advance on the shore at the height of a double-decker bus, looking awesome when viewed from Billy Sheil's coble as it negotiates one of the troughs.

Eiders swim through the ridges. The first group of puffins looks down on you from an aquatic rim and, a few moments later, is on the other side of the boat, deep in a trough, with you—almost as green as the sea—looking down upon them!

When I succeeded in getting to the Farnes, I had infinite trust in Billy Shiel and his coble, his clinker-built fishing boat, of a type named 'coble' a thousand years ago. When Alfred, a monk of Lindisfarne, was transcribing the Gospels, he lapsed from Latin into the vernacular when describing the vessel used by Jesus when putting to sea with his disciples (Matthew VIII, 23). Alfred called the boat a 'cuople'.

The Farnes lie scattered off the coast like pieces of a jig-saw. The largest island, Lindisfarne, a little to the north of the main group, is really only a demi-island, for when the tide runs out and exposes the flats it is possible to walk or drive to it on a causeway.

For me, Lindisfarne was a consolation prize when the Farnes proper were out of reach. No puffins adorned its coastline, but Cuddy's Ducks were common. In the bird book, it is listed as 'Duck, eider' but to the natives of the north-east coast, this bird is associated with St Cuthbert, the Celtic monk, who spent a prayerful life here and in his crude dwelling on the Inner Farne, a resort of saints and seabirds.

Cuthbert was not a bird-watcher as such, spending most of his time on his on his knees, looking up to heaven. Like all Celtic saints, he was in tune with nature, a brother to the birds and beasts around him. The memory of this gentle monk is linked in Northumberland with that large, blunt, marine duck, the eider.

Once, when several drake eiders were bobbing, like two-tone buoys, off the outer scars, I stood with the aforementioned old fisherman, who was smoking twist tobacco and spitting into the ebb tide. He smiled when I mentioned the old tradition that no one killed an eider, out of respect for St Cuthbert.

'Have ye tasted one?' 'No.' 'Well I wouldn't bother. It's tough and seaweedy, like a cormorant.'

He even gave me the recipe for cooking one. I must fill a saucepan with water and bring it to the boil, placing in the pan one plucked eider and one flat-iron. 'Cook 'em till the flat-iron's tender, then chuck away the eider and eat the iron!'

For my latest expedition to the Farnes, the flow-tide was 'lazy', almost imperceptible. Seahouses harbour was mirror-like, reflecting the sky. There was a sound like 'glug'. It was the precise moment at which the ebb tide became a flow.

Billy Sheil directed his boat towards the harbour mouth, thence on a two-mile voyage to the Inner Farne, which in the Celtic imagination was half way to heaven. Bede, historian of the early English Church, described the Inner Farne as 'a certain island...in the middle of the sea, not made an island like Lindisfarne by the flow of the tide...and then restored to the mainland at its ebb, but lying off several miles to the east and consequently surrounded on all sides by the deep and boundless ocean.'

Two main groups of islands are separated by Staple Sound. Far out, on the Longstone, is a lighthouse associated with Grace Darling, daughter of the keeper, who became a heroine. In 1838, she helped her father launch a boat into a stormy sea. They rescued eight people from the *Forfarshire*, which had foundered on Harcar. When the incident was publicised, Grace became a national celebrity.

Billy's coble cruised in an area of low horizons. I saw the mainland shore, with its miles of yellow sand and the blocky form of Bamburgh Castle rising from the shore like a piece of operatic scenery, with the blue ridge of Northumbrian hills far behind.

Cormorants were flying towards Big Scarcar, where they spread their sodden wings to dry and, by holding up their heads, showed off their hooked beaks, resembling a Germanic emblem.

Puffins (here called Tommy Noddies) were driven along by whirring wings. Terns, light as thistledown, doodled in the sky. But my eyes were on the swimming puffins. Their webbed feet, situated far back, were an excellent means of propulsion.

When the boat came too near a swimming bird for its comfort, the puffin took off and, in the slack air, desperately beat its wings and pattered its webbed feet on the water to gain altitude. Another puffin, in the presence of the boat, submerged without so much as a plop.

Eider drakes and duck.

Puffins are unpredictable, except among themselves. The number of birds in view fluctuates wildly, though—weather-wise—puffins do converge on the cliffs in large numbers before the onset of bad weather, whether it be a storm, heavy showers or even a sea-fret.

When we were close to the Inner Farne, the white stains on the rock near the lighthouse—stains which are often taken for seabird droppings—were seen to be in an area with few nesting sites. The white is, in fact, spent carbide from an older system of illumination at the lighthouse.

Billy brought his coble to rest by the landing in St Cuthbert's Cove, with its dash of sand, a luxury on this island. I passed near St Cuthbert's chapel, beside which an eider duck brooded eggs on its nest. Tranquillised by hormones, the eider looked for all the world like a feathered tea-cosy.

Having crossed the island, with screaming terns about me, I was soon sitting within easy viewing distance of puffins, which disported themselves on the cliff edge like day-trippers on a promenade. Here were just a few of an estimated 20,000 pairs of nesting puffins.

In their black-and-white plumage, the birds I viewed stood out against the dun colours of the rocks. At sea, the black of the bird's upperparts merged with the dark tones of the water. The white of the underparts, when seen from below—as by a fish—with the bright sky beyond, would make the puffin inconspicuous to a marine creature if it were not for the orange legs and the puffin's habit of suddenly dipping its head below the surface, an unnerving sight to marine creatures, including skin-divers.

A puffin remains underwater from twenty to forty seconds, driving itself by its wings, which normally are held half open. A diver friend mentioned the 'puffin ballet' of birds which, though somewhat cumbersome on land, dart gracefully through water, leaving trails of bubbles from air which lodged in their plumage.

My delight in puffin-watching was satisfied by some remarkably close views of the bird, which in form and colouring was in marked contrast with a nearby shag. This bird, sitting on a nest which was like a compost heap, raised its head crest and croaked with a sound like a defective plumbing system.

A pair of puffins, standing side by side among clumps of thrift and white campion, dipped their heads as they peered into the mouth of their burrow. Their triangular 'eyebrows' gave them a look of bewilderment, as though wondering what would pop out of the hole.

I was looking at a bird tuned to life in the colder-water zone of the northern hemisphere. The equivalent zone in the south is occupied by penguins, which the auks resemble superficially. They are not related.

On the Inner Farne, there was spring-cleaning to be done. Activity in one burrow was indicated by spurts of soil from an unseen puffin which was enlarging the hole, using beak and feet adorned with sharp, black claws. When the digger emerged, its white underparts were grimy.

The pair bond is maintained by billing (if not by cooing), two birds clashing their bright red, blue and yellow nebs together with a sound which carries far. Intensely curious, other puffins arrived to see what all the fuss was about.

A growling sound is heard when two puffins, locked together, bill to bill, tussle in a flurry of beak, wings and feet. Eventually, the weaker or less determined bird concentrates on escaping from the pincer-like grip of the other.

Lindisfarne.

31

The Farne Islands bear sad evidence of tracts of peaty grounds eroded by burrowing activity, by rabbits or puffins or a combination of the two. When burrows collapse, they are deserted. Wind, rain and frost complete the process of erosion which leads to mere tufts and, in due course, to bare rock, fit only for nesting cormorants.

Billy Shiel took his coble near The Pinnacles, which are bird-whitened stacks feathered with guillemots. William Howitt, a Victorian visitor, considered that the Pinnacles were 'one of the most curious and beautiful sights that I ever saw. . . [The birds] were chiefly guillemots and puffins. They seemed to be sitting erect as close as they could crowd and waving their dark wings as if for joy. . .'

In Hewitt's day, the egg-collectors 'pass from crag to crag over the roaring sea, and even from one to the other of these perpendicular isolated rocks. . . by means of a narrow board placed from one to the other, and forming a narrow bridge over such horrid gaps that the very sight of it strikes one with terror.'

Near Kittiwake Gully, puffins had gathered at the rim of the cliffs as though for committee meetings. The spongy ground of the hinterland was honeycombed by burrows.

The sun was still high as we sailed back to Seahouses. The few resident ornithologists were left to enjoy a late evening spectacle—the mass return of the puffins which had been food-gathering and the appearance of birds about to be relieved by their mates.

As a long spring day merged imperceptibly with night, the sky—tinted orangy-red by the low sun—would seem half full of puffins, circling widely, a splendid sight against the Northumbrian coast, with Bamburgh Castle like a piece of black card, propped against the sky.

Nesting Time

IF IT cannot take over an existing burrow, such as one made by a rabbit, the puffin settles down to a spell of do-it-yourself, employing its beak as a tool and its legs as shovels. The burrow may be used by the same pair of birds over several years. There is a flurry of spring-cleaning.

Billing, neck-nibbling and bill-clashing help to sustain the pair-bond. If a footloose puffin blunders into the territory, it is repulsed by a suitably aggressive posture. The last resort is an undignified scuffle.

For a puffin pair, one egg suffices. Large, and white, with faint blotchings, the egg soon becomes stained through contact with the peaty floor of the burrow. The puffin, which is long-lived, does not need more than a single egg, for it is well-concealed from predators and, being large, yields a precocious chick.

With the Atlantic puffin spread over an enormous breeding range, the time of egg-lying varies from late-March in southern colonies to the beginning of June, in the far north. Both parents incubate the egg, over a spell of about six weeks, though the female has the major share.

The length of time spent incubating varies, and may be just a few hours, the off-duty bird flying off to sea to wash, preen and feed. The sitting bird faces the circlet of light which marks the entrance to the burrow and doubtless listens to the hub-bub of the colony.

Sometimes, the egg may be left untended for a short time, the duty bird joining a group of gossiping puffins or even flying off to sea. The egg, lying in the dusty darkness of the burrow, is not chilled as would be the case if it had been laid in the open.

The first sign that eggs have hatched in a puffinry is when adult birds begin to arrive at the burrows with fish dangling from their beaks. The newly-hatched chick—the pufling—is covered with draggled down which soon dries when it is brooded. Then it becomes as fluffy as a powder-puff, being dark on the upper body and grey beneath.

The pufling struggles to its feet. In less than a week it is exercising its stubby wings, followed by leg exercises, achieved when it uses them to press its body against the end of the burrow.

When the young bird is large enough to be left, both parents gather food. The youngster increases in size and weight, greeting a returning parent with a peeping sound which betokens hunger. The adult gives a low growling.

Small fish offered to the chick are rapidly converted into body weight.

Treshnish Islands:
A Seat Among the Puffins

WE ENTERED the archipelago through the very narrow but deep channel between the Cairns, with shags showering off the rocks across our bows. . . As we passed Fladda we scanned in vain the hollow at the haven mentioned by Harvie-Brown in 1892 and by Frank (Darling) in 1937, but we were now in the midst of the skerries, weaving our course through tangle-fringed lanes of olive-green water with grey seals peering at us from many directions.

J Morton Boyd, at the Treshnish Isles, 1977.

. . . the isle of Lunga carries a multitude of nesting auks, petrels, shags and kittiwakes. They richly manure the grass on top. . . This fertilising service by sea-birds has provided pasture on large numbers of rocky islets, which although uninhabited by man are grazed by his ferried sheep, and were formerly grazed by his cattle, too.

W H Murray, 1973.

HERE (Boreray, St Kilda) the puffins breed in immense numbers, and the clouds of birds that swept past us made a sound like a whirlwind whipping a great bed of dead rushes.

Richard Kearton, 1897.

I SET my *beep-beep* alarm clock for 5 a.m. and was woken up at 4-45—by someone else's beeping alarm. Three-quarters of an hour later, with sunlight bringing a gleam to the the multi-tinted buildings of Tobermory, Isle of Mull, I was leaving harbour in a lobster boat being operated by Cameron and David, two local fishermen.

Soon I had become familiar with the routine of hauling creels, emptying creels, re-baiting creels and re-laying them where the bed of the sea is rocky, as indicated on the technicoloured screen of an echo-sounder.

After having thirteen to fourteen fathoms under the keel, we nudged into Duvaig Bay. Cameron said, brightly: 'We might touch the bottom in a minute. You'll feel a bump. Don't worry about it.'

The radio set crackled into life. 'It's the Campbelltown men chatting to themselves. They're so broad ye canna tell what they're on about.' Gulls wailed. Oystercatchers piped. The blue-black lobsters taken from the creels were mute. They were set down on the deck, out of fighting range of each other. With circumscribed movements of their scaly bodies and claws capable of giving a ferocious nip, they found sanctuary in shady places.

Victorian naturalists such as Harvie-Brown and Richard Kearton described seeing immense numbers of puffins on the Hebrides. Further south, on Ailsa Craig in the Clyde, the 1866 breeding season was so successful that some writers worried that there might be too many puffins. 'Everywhere a patch of soil is found in which it can burrow,' moaned one man. He needn't have worried. The once-vast colony went into decline because of rats, gulls and oil pollution.

At the Ascrib islands of Skye, thirty years later, Harvie-Brown saw so many puffins nesting under the turf and rocks he feared for the island itself and 'hoped that they will remain in a minority as these "comics" are quite abundant enough already...I fear that they are too much on the increase.'

I was first lured to the Treshnish group of islands by Frank Fraser Darling's book *Island Years*.

He was one of the men of scientific mind who, in the 1930s, instead of conducting research in musty laboratories, threw open the windows and let in some fresh air, following it up by taking to the wild and studying birds and animals *in situ*.

I once sat near Darling at a gathering of the British Deer Society. I did not manage to pluck up the courage to converse with him. Then he spoke to me: 'May I parisitise you?' He wanted to borrow the sugar bowl.

Darling, on the Treshnish Islands, had puffins as close neighbours; he also made observations on them during a sojourn on North Rona, the most north-westerly island of the Hebrides. Here, in 1938, he compared the large companies of cliff edge puffins with longshoremen on a harbour front. And, watching them arrive with fish, only to hang about at the mouth of the burrows for minutes on end, he asked the question: 'What are puffins thinking about all the time?'

My first glimpse of the Treshnish group was while voyaging to Staffa, celebrated for Fingal's Cave and Mendelssohn's stimulating musical impression of the place. At Tobermory, I chatted with the fisherfolk, keen to learn more about the isles from men who earned their living bobbing in boats just off-shore.

I heard of the Dutchman's Cap, the name of which could derive from those Dutch fishermen of two centuries ago who were among the first to turn herring fishing into big business.

Fourteen bullocks were once turned out on this island to graze. At the end of summer, when the owner of the cattle wished to gather them for return to Mull, he was able to catch only twelve. The other two beasts became legends in their own lifetime, wandering across the island in a semi-wild state, each weighing one and a-half tons—a deterrent to anyone who fancied himself as a toreador.

Now, with the lads from Tobermory, I was on course for the fabled Treshnish group. There was time to have a snack meal of crab meat mixed with mayonaise and spread between pieces of white bread or buttered cream crackers. Hot coffee followed.

We were soon catching bigger lobsters among the skerries. I marvelled at Cameron's skill with the boat; he delighted in taking it close to the rocks, against which the swell dissipated its energy, to drain off as a seething mass of water.

We had become part of a world of fierce tidal rips, shallows where the kelp waved like the tentacles of some giant octopus and hidden rocks which, struck by a wave, exploded in a fan of white water.

Our first sighting was of the northernmost island. West of Fladda, we had ten fathoms below us—'about four cups in the kettle'. An inter-boat conversation took place with a twenty-year-old skipper who was having little luck that day. It was an exception. 'He's been doing fine . . .'

On the weather side of Lunga, the waves broke spectacularly against Harp Rock, a resort of guillemots. I recalled a two-hour stay ashore with George, a braw Scot, who was photographed while tickling the chest of a puffin. Some of the burrows were interchangeable as dwellings between rabbits and puffins.

The facial features of a puffin leave little scope for expression beyond gaping, so the birds indicate their feelings by prescribed movements of head and wings. Serious-minded puffin-watchers use terms such as 'gape contest' and 'bowing'. The puffin also indicates its feelings by the way it walks, quite apart from that sailor-roll. The 'low profile walk' is well-named, the bird moving with its body close to the ground and horizontal rather than the normal upright stance.

Some birds were nesting among rocks and using large boulders as perches. More puffins arrived with wings vibrating like tuning forks. They displayed to each other or wandered about with dry grass in their beaks. A newly-arrived puffin shook its head rapidly, as though flicking away any surplus water. In fact, the bird was proclaiming its ownership of a particular site. A puffin slept, its body resting on the ground and its neck bent so that the triangular beak was covered by a scapular.

Homeward bound, we passed the outcropping rocks which, from a distance, gave the impression of a submarine in the process of surfacing. One rock resembled the conning tower and another the bows.

As a puffin was seen swimming on the choppy water, I chuckled at George's comment that the flattened puffin beak, with its broad band of red, suggests it has had too many drams, leading to an inflamed nose.

Mingulay:

Wild Water off the Hebrides

ON THE island of Barra, part of the great breakwater known as the Outer Hebrides, I watched a restless sea and willed the gale to fall away so that I could visit the puffins of Mingulay.

I used up my surplus nervous energy while walking along the beaches, where great waves disintegrated in flurries of foam and the gulls were wailing a Celtic lament. There was compensation for not sailing when I discovered an oystercatcher nest containing three eggs and an egg-shaped rubber ball which had been kept warm through contact with the bird's brood patch.

At Craigston, I listened to one of the few remaining corncrakes. The rasping, disyllabic *crex, crex* came from a bird skulking among the stems of yellow iris near the Catholic church. It was service time. Latecomers, speeding up, kept in step with the corncrake's urgent calling.

The view of Castlebay had been made familiar through the film version of *Whisky Galore.* Little seemed to have changed, except that now there was a free flow of whisky. The Church of Our Lady, Star of the Sea, was still perched on its ledge of rock. The tooth-like summit of the 'holy hill' of Heaval, a lump of glacier-polished gneiss, was adorned by a statue of the Madonna and Child.

The single street was the old-time mix of shops and houses. Rising from its weed-strewn islet in the bay was the ancestral castle of the MacNeill of Barra. One evening in the tourist season, two Americans were inadvertently left there. Passers-by on the mainland shore heard ghostly cries in the gloaming. The boatman recognised them for what they were and he soon rescued the visitors.

As I passed a large tourist bus, which must have fit the island road with only inches to spare, the *Mingulay Boat Song* was being rendered tinnily over the loudspeaker system:

> ...*bring her head round,*
> *Now altogether—*
> *Sailing home to Mingulay*...

The wee lasses at the information centre were happy to provide information about Mingulay and they knew the famous boat song until I asked them to sing it. Then island shyness prevailed.

The jaunty song matches the spirit of the wild water off the islands and especially those which, on the map, are like fragments of a comet's tail, with the head of the comet formed by Lewis and Harris.

I managed to hire a boat, complete with a crew of two. The owner—a MacNeill of Barra—had been reticent to take her out in view of the wild sea but by late morning conditions were moderating.

We would leave on the ebb tide and return on the flow. The outward voyage, south to Barra Head, would be to the west of the string of islands—on the open Atlantic—and we would return on the lee side. There might—or might not—be a chance to set foot on Mingulay.

What the boatman did not mention at the time was the effect of the brisk northerly wind on an already restless sea. Waves advancing on islands which spring out of deep water would collide with their predecessors, creating a flurry of water. Tide, wind, wave and an uneasy swell greeted us after we left the shelter of Vatersay, an island now tethered to Barra by a causeway.

The boat was of the lobster-fishing variety, with a wheelhouse forrard and plenty of working space behind. At times, as we entered a trough between waves, I was reminded of the wild-water study on the dustjacket of *The Cruel Sea*.

For years, I had kept Mingulay at the back of my mind as a special place—a bird island at the north-western rim of Scotland, which is also the rim of Europe. As we cruised from the sheltered water of Castlebay into a turbulent Atlantic, I reflected on my road to Mingulay, beginning with the tourist route to Oban, stopping at Dalmally for beefburger and chips.

A five hour sail, courtesy of Caledonian MacBrayne, was attended by a mounting excitement. Now was the culmination of a long journey in the company of an ex-coxwain of the lifeboat and a tall young man who (though I did not know it at the time) was part-owner of Mingulay.

A few guillemots came into view; they paddled furiously, then dived. Later, I saw the white-faced, jazzily-beaked puffin, which joined the guillemots below the waves. The boatman said that the number of seabirds, especially auks, had fallen, possibly because of over-fishing for sand-eels, a staple diet.

West of Flodday, where a natural arch tells in a graphic way of the relentless erosion of rock by the sea, I was aware that tide and wind had formed an unhappy partnership. The sun blazed in an ultramarine sky. The heaving sea sparkled with silvery highlights.

Off Lingay, where the waves were fearsome, we played hide and seek with a small fishing boat. The uneasy ocean was breaking its back on the western cliffs of Pabbay, where a 560 ft high hill has the English name of The Hoe.

From a boat dancing on a lively sea, I saw The Bishop Islands, lumps of land which have robust Norse names, terminating with -ey, which means water. An early writer, Dean Monro, mentioned that they all 'perteined to the bishoipe of the iles.' Monro mentioned that 'all thir nine iles forsaid had a chappell in every ile.'

Gannets, the 'big white birds of the herring', were diving in the bays. Fulmars gravely patrolled the area on wings which were scarcely ever flapped: they and the tail feathers were subtly adjusted to the uprushing wind which bore them effortlessly along.

Mingulay, seen across the port bow, was wedge-shaped, rising in elevation from east to west. The smooth, green hills terminated abruptly in frowning cliffs which were dark in shadow. Macphee's Hill was named after a rent-collector who was put ashore on Mingulay only to discover the islanders had died from the plague. Those in the boat, terrified of being infected, left the hapless man on the island and here he remained for a year. When Mingulay was re-settled, the owner gave him a tract of land on which to live.

The great western sea cliffs of Mingulay are among the highest in Britain, one of them—Biulacraig—having a sheer drop of almost seven hundred feet. Alexander Carmichael, in the *Crofters' Commission Report* of 1884, wrote 'there is probably no more interesting island in Britain than this island of Miuley, with its wonderful precipices, long narrow sea galleries... and marine arcades, winding their gloomy subterranean ways under the precipitous island. To boat through these galleries and arcades needs a calm sea, a good crew and a steady nerve...'

Guillemots and a Kittiwake.

We experienced a short, violent storm. The water was as dark as Stephen's ink. From under the waterproofed hood of my anorak I saw a turbulance of water and the fixed stares of puffins which breasted it. The wind shrieked. The water became a confused mass of short, white-topped waves. The puffins which speckled the water seemed more suspicious of the boat than of the elements.

When the dark clouds passed, we were in calmer water, looking at Barra Head, the southernmost point of the isle of Berneray. This formidable headland is situated fifty-four miles from Ardnamurchan, the most westerly point on the Scottish mainland, and ninety-five miles from the Irish coast. A lighthouse is perched near the edge of a 645 ft high cliff.

The sea was speckled with puffins and guillemots. Flurries of kittiwakes enlivened the faces of the dark cliffs. Fulmars, which arrived at Barra Head in 1899, as part of their astonishing spread from the St Kilda archipelago, were on patrol.

Barra Head is, acccording to W H Murray, 'a place of storm, of unceasing wind.' Spray has been tossed to a height of over six hundred feet and small fish deposited on the grass at the top of Skate Point. The lighthouse, built by the Stevenson family in the 1828s, has the visual effect of an exclamation mark.

David Stevenson, when prospecting for a good site for the lighthouse, reported on the wretched condition of the inhabitants of Berneray, who lived in houses of the 'but and ben' type.

They had tuned their lives to the wild elements. Three years later, when the lighthouse was under construction, using granite quarried on Berneray, Robert Stevenson reported: 'Such is the violence of the wind in this station from the lofty and abrupt form of the island that the temporary buildings occupied by the artificers engaged in the works have been temporarily unroofed.'

Barra Head lighthouse, which is visible for 35 miles, is now operated automatically; the attendants arrive by helicopter. The lorry which ran a shuttle service between the jetty and the cliff-top lighthouse for many years had to negotiate such steep gradients that only first gear was used.

We turned northwards and the sheltered eastern coastline of Mingulay came into view. We exchanged awesome cliffs and deep shadows for sun-drenched sward and dune. The boatman headed for one side of a half-moon shaped bay. He pointed out the two habitable buildings, one being a haven for the shepherds when they landed on Mingulay to attend to their sheep in summer.

The boat was brought against smooth rock to the north of the bay, in an area known as Rubh' an Droma. A hooded crow took flight. A few big gulls gave sniggering cries. And I came under the the gaze of puffins.

The folk of Mingulay, in their isolation, depended on 'sea fowl' to augment whatever crops they could grow—potatoes, small oats, rye and barley. A crofter might have two or three cows and a pony. He used peat as fuel.

The boatman said: 'Everyone knows the people on St Kilda lived largely on seabirds. So did the people of Mingulay, but you scarcely ever hear it mentioned...' Seabirds were inclined to be oily. The islander removed as much oil as possible when preparing them. If a broth was being made, more oil might be skimmed off the surface. Broth was thickened up using oatmeal.

The fowlers of this island were able to seek birds or eggs without the use of ropes; they simply scrambled about the gneiss rock, finding plenty of foot and hand holds. If a man of Mingulay slipped, it was certain death amid the flurry of white water at the base of the cliff.

Tales were told of the bravery of such a man, a *gingich,* who was adroit at leaping from and back onto a sea-tossed boat as it lay off such a mighty stack as Lianamul.

The people of Mingulay boiled puffins for hours at a time or they roasted a puffin at the peat fire. Hearing of the Mingulanian taste for sea-parrots, I was reminded of the, already related, account of how to cook an eider duck. Boil it with a flat-iron until the iron is tender. Then eat the flat iron and throw the eider duck away.

J A Harvie-Brown, a naturalist who visited the Hebridean island of Mingulay just over a century ago, noted that 'the puffin has complete hold over the whole upper crust...Later in the year the whole surface is one sticky compound of mud and dung, feathers, bad eggs and defunct young puffins, ankle-deep or deeper—waiting perhaps to be scraped away some day from the rocky area on which it rests, and be spread far and near over the worn-out pastures by future generations of farmers—truly a filthy if a fruitful compost.'

The fulmar was prized both for its flesh and also for the oil it yielded—oil that kept the household lamps burning on a winter night.

Fachaich (fatlings, or young shearwaters) were a delicacy. So many were gathered up that the flesh was accepted in lieu of rent by the MacNeill, who voyaged from Barra a fortnight before Lammas and stayed on the island for about a month. One account states that the laird returned to Barra with twenty barrels tightly packed with birds.

The flow-tide pushed us back to Castlebay, under the gaze of pouting puffins and a few guillemots. Puffins were sparse. The boatman shook his head and remarked: 'In the old days, if you landed on Mingulay, the air was black with 'em.'

PUFFINS AMONG THE SEA PINKS AND WHITE CAMPION.

GANNETRY ON THE CLIFFS AT NOSS, SHETLAND.
Puffins nest in burrows driven along the rim of the cliffs.

Above: Muckle Flugga and the Outstack—the most northerly rocks in Britain—as seen from Hermaness, the location of one of Shetland's largest colonies of puffins. *Below:* Puffin at its burrow on Noss.

David Binns.

On the previous two pages: The Farne Islands, off the Northumbrian coast, showing shag, guillemot, cormorant, eider, puffin, black-backed gull, kittiwake, Arctic tern and grey seal. The centrepiece is Longstone Lighthouse.
Above: The great black-backed gull, which plucks puffins from the sky and has the gruesome knack of turning a bird inside out when eating it.

Left: Arctic shore: an effigy on Grimsey Island, off the northern coast of Iceland.
Below: Puffins in the hard northern sunlight.

EVENING SUNLIGHT AT HUSAVIK, ICELAND.
The harbour is being stirred up by the fast boat taking a party
of bird-watchers to Puffin Island, in the Arctic Ocean.

Cape Wrath:

A Place for Turning

TO REACH Faraid Head, near Durness, where puffins have a major mainland presence, and the watcher does not have to suffer from sea-sickness, I walked around the bay and entered a desert zone, with shifting sand as fine as that in an hour-glass.

Life was infused into this Scottish desert by the whistles and chacks of wheatears. At the tip of the headland, kittiwakes called and shags sat morosely on their nests. Off-shore stacks were tiered and whitened, resembling wedding-cakes, 'iced' by guano.

The puffinry lay where wind-blown sand had solidified and become thatched with grasses. Naturally terraced grassland swept down to the sea. Puffin burrows were everywhere. A few off-duty or non-breeding birds exchanged pleasantries in the sunlight. It amazed me that such a mainland colony could flourish when it must have innumerable visits by bird-watchers.

I watched a bird preening, using a gland situated just above the bird's tail, providing a supply of oil which, spread on the feathers, keeps them waterproof.

I waited near the *Cape Wrath Hotel* for the ferryboat which, powered by outboard engine, crosses the firth, breasting a flow tide and picking its way carefully around sandbanks on the ebb. The ferryman is idle when the tide is low. So are the seals, which haul themselves on to the banks or simply wait for the outflowing tide to maroon them.

The wooded shore of the Cape Wrath peninsula, a mere half mile away, belied the appearance of the wild country beyond.

Or its status as a naval gunnery range. A notice expressed it forcibly: 'It is dangerous to stray from the road or to enter this area owing to unexploded shells.'

From the south, Cape Wrath is approached by a long, rough walk. I took the easy route, stepping into the ferry for a brief voyage—a mere nothing in comparison to those of the Norse seafarers who named Sutherland ('the south land') and Cape Wrath ('the turning point').

A road eleven miles long ends with the famous lighthouse. On my first visit, our mini-bus (which had been taken across the firth by raft) splashed through the Daill Ford. The driver said, cheerfully: 'A friend of mine ran over a salmon.' Now there's a Bailey Bridge.

I had a feeling that the telegraph poles beside the road were much shorter than the average. Perhaps they had sunk in peat or were just keeping their heads down against the time the Navy began to lob shells into this area. It was tempting—though only for an instant—to cross the range and make a start on watching puffins on the range of high cliffs extending westwards to Cape Wrath. I was deterred by a factor which leads to only scattered activity—the errant naval shell!

Where the Lewisian gneiss has its final flourish, a lighthouse was built by Robert Stevenson and his family. In 1798, Stevenson's gale-tossed ship lost part of its rigging and he was obliged to bear away. 'The wind got to such a height that we were afraid to keep out longer in case she should be carried past the Orkneys altogether and so have no harbour to leeward.'

That storm lasted for over a fortnight.

To Walter Scott (1814) the north-west termination of mainland Scotland was 'this dead Cape'. He saw a pair of large eagles and lamented there was no rifle handy. 'They are, I suppose, little disturbed here for they showed no great alarm.'

I made for the Torridonian sandstone, a mile or two eastwards of the Cape, where the largest seabird colonies are to be found. Initially, I followed a path to Kervaig, a delightful cove. A tumult of foam-crested waves was backed by a wind coming straight from the Arctic, with no intermediate land to slow it down. It provided a spectacular show under a blue sky.

A bonxie tugged at something on the beach, took to the air half-heartedly, changed its mind and returned to the object of its interest. Gannets were commuting between their nesting islands and the shoals of fish. Seeing the rusty form of an oil-tanker, not too far from land, sent a chill down my spine at the thought of the consequences of an accidental spillage. Oil slicks not only clog the feathers of seabirds; they cause the plumage to lose its waterproofing. Auks like the puffin appear to associate smooth patches of oil on the water with shoals of fish. They make for them.

I was on a coastline of superlatives, featuring a grand cliffscape. Here was Cleit Dubh (at 850 ft the highest cliff on the British mainland) and Clo Mor (600 ft). There was soil into which the puffins might burrow. These nesting places were situated dizzily on steep ground close to the cliffs. Incoming birds were supported by an updraught of such force that the fulmars had almost forgotten how to flap, using their considerable gliding skill most of the time.

The cliff path led me through a pink-and-green environment: the pink of sandstone, the green of grass, well fertilised by bird droppings and unmown by sheep. A promontory of pink rock was a high perch for razorbills and yet more puffins, which stood with grave expressions as, far below, the waves spent themselves against rock with dull thuds.

I was now looking down on part of the largest mainland colony of puffins in Britain—a nesting area with up to 50,000 pairs of birds. As in other puffinries, comparatively few of the residents were visible, for it was afternoon.

Puffins were flying in with fish-food for their young. The number of fish clasped in a puffin's beak reflected good feeding. In some years, when the fish stocks are low, the chicks do not put on the fat that is vital to their well-being and many of them die.

Puffins were running the gauntlet of great black-backed gulls. The flight of a puffin is powerful but direct and the big gulls have become skilful at plucking them out of the sky. A luckless puffin is carried to the nearest clifftop, here to be killed, the body being pecked open and shaken inside out. When the gull has finished dining, all that remains are the inedible bits of puffin—including the skin.

I was tempted to stay until evening, when many puffins which are ready to fly to sea adopt their 'moth flight', a low-speed affair, the body arched and the head angled down.

Puffins also follow the broad circular flight, which has been compared with a wheel, flying partly over land and partly over the sea. It takes place when a colony has been disturbed but may also occur spontaneously, lasting for long periods, though it is unlikely that a particular bird stays with it for the duration. Birds on the sea may be stimulated to join the wheel, and it is from the wheel that many a puffin drops down to its burrow.

Any marauding gulls find it difficult to take birds from a wheel and usually go for solitary puffins.

I heard the screaming of kittiwakes. My nostrils twitched with the musty tang of bird droppings. Guillemots had the numerical superiority. Some of the largest guillemot colonies in Britain are situated on the cliffs and stacks between Handa and the western coastline of Orkney.

After the heady experience of walking by the sea, in the company of thousands of screaming or croaking seabirds, I entered the silent wilderness of the moors. My feet were muffled by peat or sphagnum. A whistle, low and sad, came from a golden plover which stood on tiptoe to watch me passing.

Orkney:

Low Green Isles

I SAIL north from Aberdeen, in the P & O ferry *St Sunniva,* which the brochure describes as 'a floating hotel'. The weather is cloudy, somewhat cool. A shaft of sunlight illuminates Duncansby Head, at which stage of the voyage I look across the grey corrugations of the Pentland Firth—and see Orkney.

Mainland unfolds as a large, green island. The Orcadian roads are ruler-straight. The Orcadian landscape is divided up by miles of posts and wire, with few walls. Herds of cattle live naturally, in social groupings, each group with an attendant bull and some new calves to speak of its virility.

In Kirkwall, I observe to a shopkeeper that June is supposed to be one of the sunniest and driest months. He does not commit himself, merely remarking, in a semi-quizzical way, 'where on earth did you read that?' A visitor from Caithness speaks, in the lounge, of the clarity of Orcadian air and how at night, 'the stars seem so low you feel you can reach up and pluck some.'

My first puffin hunt was to Noup Head on Westray. I joined a Loganaire flight (in an Islander twin-engined aircraft). My fellow passengers were a Westray woman, a schoolteacher and the local chiropodist, who that day also intended to exercise his skill as a dentist.

It was a smooth if noisy flight. The aircraft flew as purposefully as a bumble bee, crossing more low green islands and a waveless sea for a landing on grass at the north end of Westray. I had telephoned ahead for a taxi to take me to Noup Head and its bird cliffs. It was not that I was feeling lazy—merely that time was limited before the return flight to Kirkwall at 3 p.m.

The genial taximan, who was also the garage proprietor, had an old Austin which must have been familiar with the route—a metalled road which became a roughish track to the lighthouse. The Council had fenced off a prominent area beside the road as a dumping place for old cars.

The taximan turned off the track, did a neat circuit on grass and courteously opened the door to permit me to descend beside the lighthouse and near the cliff edge. He led me to where the big slabs of rock were tinted orange and grey by lichen.

Finding a good vantage point, I looked along the flagstone cliff. Every ledge had its rows of birds, mainly guillemots of the dark northern type, with kittiwakes either sitting on their nests or prettily engaged in preening their feathers. Other kittiwakes swirled and shouted their names.

The guillemots had turned away from the sea, and appeared to cling to the sloping ledges like passengers on the slanting deck of a stricken liner. They would have eggs beneath them. Nesting is a precarious time for the ledge-nesting auks.

Before departing, the taximan pointed out some grey seals on the outlying rocks. He ignored my request for details of how much money I owed him. Och, but it would do later. If I was at his garage by 2-40 he would take me back along the dreary road to the airport.

Then he was gone. Och, but there's lots of time, I thought. And it's all doonhill!

Seeing the massed seabirds, I marvelled at the high productivity of the sea around Orkney. That sea abounds in summer plankton, attracting small shoaling fish and, in turn, the seabirds. I had heard grim tales of a fish shortage on Shetland. The sand-eel population had slumped and with it some of the large colonies of terns and auks. Orkney did not appear to have experienced it—yet.

I crossed the sheep-cropped grassland of the cliff-top and was harassed by oystercatchers which had the defence of chicks. For an hour or two, while passing through a succession of territories, I had the shrill piping of the parent birds in my ears. When the local bonxies showed interest, I was glad I was carrying a stick, for I could raise it above my head.

The turf was spangled with flowers—with sea pinks, squill, orchids, pansies and daisies.

A score of black guillemots (tysties) stood or rested on their tarsii at the rim of the rocks overlooking the sea. I saw the black plumage, white wings and coral red feet. The birds, when agitated, gave a thin whistling call. My snack meal was near a natural rock arch, buttressed by cliffs dotted with reclining fulmars and patchy with sea pinks in full bloom. I located a few puffins.

The taximan conveyed the chiropodist/dentist and ourselves to the airport. I happily paid £6 for the transport. The pilot having to go to Papa Westray, I was taken on the shortest air route in the world—a brief hop across the sound between two islands and a touch-down in a field as lush as a meadow. Mail was put aboard.

Pleasantries between the pilot and airfield staff—a young man—took less than a minute and then we were awa', in brightening conditions, the pitch of the engine rising and settling down to a drone as we cleared the field to fly low, over a few farms, a ruined church in a large burial ground and eventually across the coast, where the sea had nibbled at the cliffs, producing deep indentations known as geo's.

Another day, a steady climb led me to Costa Head, the reputed nesting place of puffins. I did not see any, partly because I did not want to risk life and limb approaching the cliff edge on a grassy slope. I had to be content to watch fulmars trimming their wings

Oystercatchers and sea pinks.

and tails to the updraught and gliding effortlessly.

I joined one of David Lea's parties, mainly because he included a trip to Ward's Hill cliffs and mentioned puffins among the bird species to be seen. The bus squeezed its way along the road to its ending in a rough farmyard. We made a circuitious trip (round three sides of a meadow, to avoid trampling grass) and cut across the moor to the cliffs, where puffins were soon located, far down, at a place where a grassy slope overlies a rim of rock. Three birds only were visible.

At Stromness, I watched the ferry being cast off and saw a red glow just beyond the hill, where the sun was setting, though there was much mist and cloud. After a fitful sleep, I awoke to a grey world, with visibility down to a few hundred yards. Breakfast was served in a cheerful restaurant. Then I glanced out to see, faintly, some features of Aberdeen harbour. The crew turned the huge ferry in the harbour and then reversed it, yard by yard, to the P & O mooring.

Said the purser, just before I left the ship: 'The first time I went to Orkney, I was ashore in Stromness, feeling strange. Yet everyone seemed to know me. The best part of the Orkney Islands is—the people!'

Shetland:

Land of the Simmer Dim

IT WAS an uneasy dawn, with light seeping into a moist world. Layers of cloud, in various shades of grey, were like washes applied by an energetic water-colourist. The *St Clair*, over ten hours out of Aberdeen, had spent the brief night flirting with a north-easterly swell, a persistent wind blowing around an anti-cyclone which was centred on Scandinavia.

I was *en route* to Lerwick in Shetland, which has a hundred islands and 2,500 freshwater lochs, a scattering of voes, huge sea cliffs—and lots of puffins.

North of Dunnet Head, the most northerly point on the British mainland, the weather is a never-ending topic. The Shetland climate, like the Shetlanders themselves, is not inclined towards extremes. A mildish summer is followed by a mildish winter.

Yet, said a man at the rail of *St Clair*, there had been extremes. Before Christmas, he had walked on snow so dry it squeaked under his feet. And less than a fortnight before I met him, he had seen a bikini-clad girl helping with the 'peats'. In Shetland, it is wise to sunbathe wearing a jumper.

The *St Clair* entered the channel between Mainland and Bressay towards the end of a two hundred mile voyage. Beyond Bressay, and yet appearing to be of the same land mass, was the wedge-shape of Noss, its eastern cliffs soaring to about six hundred feet.

There was endless bird traffic—gannet, guillemot, shearwater, puffin—all coping with the wind in their distinctive ways.

The *St Clair* came slowly to rest at Lerwick ('clay creek'), where a replica of a Norse longboat rode high in the water. With puffins on my mind, I drove off the ferry and, shortly afterwards, on to the red, white and blue ferry operating across half a mile of water to Bressay.

One of the ferrymen told me of the night a visiting skipper left Lerwick for the oil-rigs, which lay due east. He set the appropriate course, but had forgotten all about the isle of Bressay. His craft ran up the beach.

I was overswept by puffin-fever and did not stop for rest or food. All that mattered was that I should catch the wee ferry across the sound to the Isle of Noss, the name of which (a Norse name, of course) means 'a point of rock'. It is a bare island. The tallest plant is said to be the rhubarb in the garden at Gungstie, where naturalists stay and the ferry attendant is based.

My crossing was by inflatable boat, with a young woman at the controls. We zig-zagged across the sound in deference to the eider families.

At the Point of Harvie, I stood in a natural rock garden, stained by a carpet of sea pinks varied by flowers of yellow hue and by the deep red of the Shetland variety of red campion. A drystone wall, built to restrain domestic animals at the edge of the fearsome cliffs, was now badly gapped. I chanced to look over the cliff and was spotted by one of the great black-backed gulls nesting on Cradle Holme. The bass baritone voice of the gull joined the more strident seabird chorus.

I looked through a stratum of seabirds to where shags occupied the large ledges near the sea. Against a chorus of raucous voices came a powerful soloist, the Shetland wren. Where the topmost ledge was rank with vegetation, the head of a puffin was in view, the rest of the bird being tucked away in its nesting burrow.

The puffin appeared to be debating with itself whether or not to fly. Tammie Norie—as the Shetlander calls the puffin—seemed apprehensive, as well it might be with the great black-backed gulls nesting nearby.

The puffin, having mulled over the circumstances, during a short busy spell of preening, decided to fly, moving on short, relatively broad wings. There was no question of gliding; it beat its wings furiously and, meanwhile, contrived to look over its shoulder, as though scared that I might be following.

A great black-backed gull, buoyant with the upward rush of air from the cliffs, finds the wheeling of many puffins off-putting but selects a solitary bird. If the puffin is aware of an impending attack, it takes instant action, dropping into the sea. A gull which approaches from above and behind has the advantage of the puffin's 'blind spot' and, outflying the puffin, grasps it and flies with its still-struggling prey to a place where it may be languidly consumed.

A lively puffin has been known to escape from the bill of a big gull or even from the spot where the gull has taken it for final despatch.

Shetland had been suffering from a scarcity of small-fish food, a shortage associated with over-fishing for species which in the old days had no commercial value. Sand-eels, caught through the agency of electronic gadgetry, had been taken for conversion into fish meal. And sand-eels are a staple of the puffins and Arctic terns.

A vast puffin colony on Rost, off Norway, had an estimated one million inhabitants but was reduced by three-quarters, almost certainly through an over-kill by fishermen of sand-eels, sprats and herring.

My last view of the puffins of Noss was of birds standing in the sunshine on the stones of the old wall. A bird preened, distributing oil from the preen gland to keep its plumage waterproofed. Another puffin arrived with a white feather clasped in its beak. The others simply stood and returned my gaze. Or were assembled in small groups, as though discussing the gossip of the day. I watched a seaborne puffin preening and was impressed by the time it took to attend to its feathers. When it rolled on its side, it exposed a greater area of white underparts.

I inched my way over a slab of sandstone, in full view of the Noup of Noss. The breeze delivered the tang of seabirds. Another inch or two, and I was looking into space—to where the sea, hundreds of feet below me, thudded against cliffs that, higher up, were providentially weathered into horizontal ledges, ideal for gannets. Ledge after ledge had its solemn brooding birds.

Far, far to the north—and several ferry rides away—lay the island of Unst and the great bird-cliffs of Hermaness. Standing in a 'thin' wind, as the last of the ferries ironed out waves in Bluemill Sound, I watched strings of gannets and auks, either departing for or returning to the rich fishing grounds of the east.

I motored through Unst, playing the 'most northerly' game. At Haroldswick stood the most northerly church in Britain—not an ancient greystone edifice dedicated to one of the Celtic saints but a Methodist chapel. North of the chapel, the RAF station and a rounded bay called Nor Wick, was Skaw, the most northerly house.

To reach it I crossed moorland where great skuas—the notorous bonxies—lay on dry knolls and a few Arctic skuas let off their surplus nervous energy to the accompaniment of fiendish cries. The bonxies were languid; the Arctics uttered their mewing calls as they pursued each other at speed.

Skaw was solitary, remote, about 180 miles to the north of John o' Groats. The house appeared grey-roofed, white-walled, with some liberal applications of red paint to the door and gate. An up-turned boat, redundant as a boat, now served as the ample roof of an outbuilding. Nothing goes to waste on Shetland.

I was now ready for an expedition to Hermaness. Heading north-westwards, I saw one of the fairest views. The road passed between Loch of Cliff, which is composed of fresh water, and Burra Firth, an arm of the sea. The golfball-like radome of the station on Saxa Vord was complimented on the other side of the firth by a huddle of white buildings, from which the lighthouse on Muckle Flugga was serviced.

An American who planned to visit Hermaness looked at the sky and remarked: 'I'm sure going to take my poncho.' He strode ahead. I did not see him again!

Hundreds of common orchids stood to attention among the straggling grasses of a hillside near the lighthouse buildings. A moorland track lay beyond. Here was typical hill ground, with peat and heather giving way at altitude to drier, grassy expanses.

Hermaness Hill, long famed for its skuas and seabird city, is not a difficult hill to climb. The moorland tract holds about a thousand pairs of bonxies and perhaps two hundred and fifty pairs of Arctic skuas. The ground beyond the summit slopes gently to cliffs and stacks where seabirds congregate. T A Coward, a famous or-nithologist, who visited Hermaness in 1927, wrote of ledges like 'congested districts', the air filled with 'graceful flying fowl' and countless swimming birds dotting the waves.

Puffins and great black-backed gulls.

On the day of my visit, Hermaness was hard and dry—dusty, indeed—after weeks of unaccustomed drought. The vegetation crackled under my feet. Bonxies made the air crackle with their gutteral voices.

The northern sky clouded. Some raindrops fell on a grateful earth. Hermaness Hill seemed to cleave the storms but eventually was overwhelmed. I scurried to a wooden hut, a conspicuous object on this treeless landscape. The timbers creaked as they took the strain of the storm. It was in the hut that I saw my first puffin of the day—a painting of its head and shoulders, part of a collection of high-class drawings and sensible graffiti.

The cloud mass thinned. A few tatters of cloud remained and were soon swept away. I stepped out of the hut to find myself under a powder-blue sky. The most northerly skylark in Britain rose like a feathered helicopter, brimming over with song.

I strode to where tumbling cliffs confronted the Atlantic. A line of stacks and skerries had a fringe of foam. My eyes sought and

71

found Outstack, or North Stack, Britain's most northerly piece of rock. The much better-known Muckle Flugga, rising to two hundred feet, gave the impression it was leaning against tide and wind. The lighthouse appeared to be the only true vertical. The rock was given a white hue from the ivory bodies of nesting gannets. Guano had splashed the rock. The Flugga might have been hastily whitewashed.

On Hermaness, puffins adorned the screes and grassy slopes. Far below were the guillemots, packed on ledges in seemingly disordered array, but with each bird mindful of its own little space, which it was ever ready to defend with a jab of the bill or a noisy growling.

Razorbills abounded on broken cliff faces. Shags had built their compost-heaps on the big ledges near the sea. And everywhere, kittiwakes clouded the air and pitched their voices high, so that they were clearly heard above the avian hub-bub and the roaring sea.

A PUFFIN MAY NEST AMONG ROCKS BUT IS MOST
FREQUENTLY ASSOCIATED WITH BURROWS IN SOFT
GROUND ON CLIFF SLOPES.

Farne Island Puffins.

David Binns.

Opposite page:
STUDIES BY DAVID
BINNS OF PUFFINS
NESTING ON THE
FARNE ISLANDS, OFF
THE NORTHUMBRIAN
COAST, WHERE THE
POPULATION IS
THRIVING.

This page:
THE FARNE ISLANDS
FORM A SUITABLE
NESTING PLACE FOR
THE EIDER. PICTURED
HERE IS THE FEMALE
OF THE SPECIES.

Above: Puffins in a small gossiping group on the Farnes. The concentration of puffins on this famous group of islands off the north-east coast of England has led to considerable erosion of the soil and vegetation.
Top, right: This signpost on Grimsey, off the north coast of Iceland, signifies the Arctic Circle. Grimsey offers the puffin a wide choice of nesting sites, from high cliffs to rocky terrain at sea level.
Right: A kittiwake at its nest on the Northumbrian coast. This lively, ocean-going gull is often found in areas where puffins are common.

SOME OTHER SEA BIRDS. *Above:* Cormorants nesting on a rock on the Farne group. Longstone lighthouse is seen in the distance. *Opposite page:* Gannets, which in Scotland are 'the white birds of the herring'.
These studies were made on Bass Rock, in the Firth of Forth, 313 ft high and a mile in circumference. If an ancient passage in the Anglo-Saxon poem *The Seafarer* refers to the colony, it has existed for at least 1,200 years.

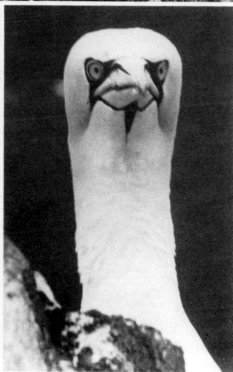

Above: AN ARMY LANDING CRAFT DELIVERS SUPPLIES TO HIRTA, ONE OF THE ST KILDA GROUP. THE PUFFIN ISLAND OF DUN IS SEEN ACROSS VILLAGE BAY.

Below: AT THE ST KILDA ARMY BASE. THE SOCIAL CENTRE IS NAMED AFTER THE PUFFIN.

St Kilda:

By Gemini to Dun

THERE remained St Kilda, the famous cluster of islands far to the west, 'at the edge of the world'. My first view of St Kilda had been during an Icelandair flight from Reykavik to Glasgow. I was dozing after a light meal. The amplified voice of the pilot mentioned, 'for anyone who might be interested', that we were passing near 'the isles of St Kilda'.

My sudden backward movement at the news brought a responsive grunt from the woman in the seat behind who suffered instant compression of the knees. And there, far below, were the isles of my dreams: Hirta and Boreray, with their satellites—Soay, Dun and the Stacks.

Dun? In the context of the western isles of Scotland it is a mere speck off Hirta, the main island in the St Kilda group. Having been accepted as a member of a National Trust for Scotland working party, I sailed to St Kilda happy to know that there would be both work and play.

Our boat passed close to Borerary, where puffins co-exist with sheep on the steep grassy slopes. The grazing of the sheep not only trims the vegetation but consolidates the ground.

At St Kilda, the puffin population can be divided into three, with nesting colonies on Dun, Boreray and Soay. There is no precise figure for Dun's population, but it is somewhere between 60,000 and 80,000 pairs.

An evening walk brought me to a point overlooking Dun, the mile long rocky ridge which was once part of Hirta but had a channel driven through by the tides. Dun still gives protection to the Bay and when a storm rages, sheets of spray may overtop the island. The southern rocks are grey and seamed, like the skin of a reptile.

Dun welcomes seabirds, having ledges, stacks, peaty areas and boulder slopes. The sharp crest of the island divides the southern side, where the cliffs are up to five hundred feet high, from the northern side, an area of steeply shelving slopes, riddled with puffin burrows.

Writers about St Kilda devoted much space to puffins. The early accounts tell of vast numbers of birds, that of Macaulay in 1764 telling that 'sometimes while on the wind [they] involve everything below them in darkness, like a small cloud of locusts, in another country.'

Mackenzie, in 1905, wrote: 'There is not a suitable spot anywhere which does not swarm with them. Everywhere you see them in thousands, while at the same time the air is full of them coming and going.' The islanders slew puffins by the thousand, using their flesh as food and collecting their feathers for sale to the factor.

A stone of feathers was plucked from no less than four hundred and fifty puffins and the factor was at one time being supplied with two hundred stone annually. 'The feathers of other birds are mixed with them, but Puffins are by far the greatest producers,' noted Elliott in 1895. By 1903, they seemed even more numerous. Wiglesworth accounted for this by the fact they were no longer secured for the sake of their feathers.'

By 1894, puffins on Boreray and Soay were so common that their burrows were destroying the pastures where large numbers of sheep had been grazed.

Ornithologists of the 1930s—Lack, Nicholson and Fisher among them—were impressed by the huge number of puffins.

James Ferguson-Lee confided in his diary in 1948: 'During the day, the air above Dun continued to be a whirling twisting mass of birds—uncountable thousands...On Dun, the entire grassy slope was found to be one mass of burrows...Adults flying round overhead and over the sea in hundreds and thousands, all forming one huge unbroken circle...'

The Army, who maintain a small garrison on Hirta, delivered our little group to the island of Dun (pronounce it 'Doon'). We did so in style. An immense fork-lift truck picked up a Gemini inflatable and lumbered with it to the sea, placing it gently on the water. We were taken, three or four at a time, from the side of the pier, across a puffin-speckled Village Bay, to where a white rope extended down the rocks and provided the only handy way to a huge puffinry. Our approach was by way of natural tunnel and we landed near the inlet known as Seilg Geo.

When my turn came to use the rope, I found myself in a natural garden. From cracks in the volcanic rocks—rocks which had a dull red appearance, as though they had set in terror—grew a miscellany of salt-tolerant plants, including thrift and white campion.

I advanced through an area where sheep had been absent for many years and plants had grown unchecked. Common sorrel formed a mini-jungle. In its lusty growth on sheep-free land and under grey St Kildan skies, it would hide the activities of the puffins from sightseeing naturalists or natural predators. Lesser celandine was common. Scentless mayweed appeared in every view. I saw the dead stalks of angelica.

Old puffin areas were still spongy and those in current use showed exposed earth which had been pounded flat by webbed feet. It was wise to ignore such areas or a thoughtlessly placed foot would go through the roof of a burrow. In some areas, now deserted, it was like looking at the remains of a forgotten city.

'Puffin vegetation', mentioned in the guide book, was stated to be plant communities modified by the manurial, burrowing and trampling effects of the birds.

St Kilda wrens were common. It astonished me, while sitting on the crest of the island, with seabirds all around, to hear a cascade of sharp, clear notes from a cock wren and to find that the wee bird was perched on a lichen-encrusted boulder, within a few feet of a puffin.

I walked to the limit of the permitted area, beyond which puffins filled the air with the density of bees around a hive. Village Bay was speckled with off-duty birds.

I sat in the sunlight and watched a puffin from close range as it posed on a rock festooned with orange lichen. From the parrot-like beak were draped half a dozen sand-eels, which gleamed in the bright light. A fellow member of our party said: 'It's nice to watch another species that doesn't feel it has to be working all day long. The puffins don't seem to do anything.'

So I watched a group of puffins. They were busy—in their way. One puffin stretched its wings after landing and used the wings to assist its progress up a shallow slope. I was reminded of film I had seen of penguins coming ashore in the Antarctic.

Another puffin was preening systematically. A gossiping group had formed at the cliff edge. None of the birds seemed to move, but when I watched with special care, they were seen to be shuffling about. Their positions changed—by the minute.

Several puffins arrived with silvery fish, mainly sand-eels, draped from their beaks. They lost no time in going underground. Various species of fish are counted as food, but some are more nutritious than others. Sand-eels and fry come into this category. Less important are rockling and whiting.

Whether in flight or on the ground, puffins were forever looking over their shoulders. The few local pairs of great black-backed gulls are believed to take over 2,000 puffins in the nesting season.

Dun continued to fascinate me during my St Kildan sojourn. On my evening walk to Ruaival, I looked across the Sound at the massed seabirds. An even better view of the island was to be had from the Mistress Stone, where the wind was so strong I encountered Vertical Take-off Starlings. Birds which had been feeding young at the nests in the jumble of boulders emerged normally but shot upwards when caught by the furious draught from the cliff.

From the highest point of Hirta, near the remains of a crashed military aircraft and not far from the Cleit at the Edge of the World, was a tantalising glimpse of far-off islands—just a smudge on the horizon, marking out the Flannans, with their several thousand breeding pairs of puffins.

Atlantic Seal.

The Fledglings Depart

FOR WEEKS, the young puffin sees little of the outside world—just the circlet of daylight which is the entrance to the burrow and through which the parent birds arrive hastily, with food.

For forty days and forty nights, the pufling does little else but put on weight and defacate. In the snug recess of the burrow, it is safe from marauding gulls. A clicking call heralds the arrival of an adult bird with food; the young bird responds with a peeping call. At first, the parents are finicky feeders but eventually the whole meal is dumped in the burrow, to be eaten as desired.

On moonless nights, when predator birds are inactive, the pufling shuffles to the mouth of the burrow and exercises its wings.

Iceland:
Land of Fire and Water

Great black-backed gull pursues a puffin.

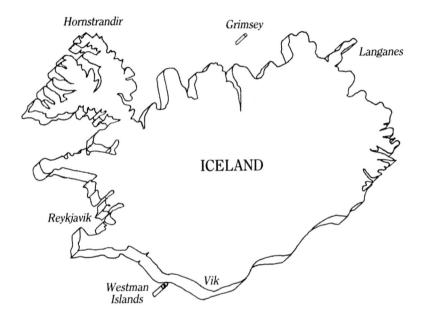

Hornstrandir

Grimsey

Langanes

ICELAND

Reykjavik

Vik

Westman
Islands

AT GLASGOW Airport, the hiss of rain did not vary from minute to minute. 'Och, it's just a wee shower,' said the taxi driver. Gulls were admiring their reflections in puddles.

A DC-8 of Icelandair was being fussed over by airport workers after its flight from Copenhagen. It would take less than two hours to reach Iceland. Before there was a regular air link, a steamer from the Clyde took four days to complete the crossing, sailing in the lee of the Hebrides before passing the Butt of Lewis into the full fury of the North Atlantic.

Long before that, Irish monks—the original cockleshell heroes—cast themselves on to the ocean in boats made of hide, braced by wood and powered by the wind. Divine insurance cover was provided. Bottles of holy water were carried. The Christian saints arrived on an island so different from their native land. Here were fire and water. Volcanoes flared. Huge waterfalls roared out like prophets in the wilderness.

St Brendan and his companions, on a voyage which took them to North America, remembered Iceland as 'a large and misty island in the ocean . . . with misty clouds above it, and a great smoke issuing from its summit'. The peak of the mountain was 'unclouded and shooting up flames into the sky which it drew back again to itself so that the mountain was a burning pyre . . . '

Men from the viks or creeks of Norway, using long, lean seagoing craft with striped sails and dragonesque prows, began the Viking Age. Ingolfur Arnarson, the first true settler, had no intention of returning home. He took with him the sacred, elaborately carved pillars from his high seat at home.

On reaching south-west Iceland, he tossed them into the sea, announcing that he would make his home where the pillars were washed up. Ingolfur Arnarson found them in a bay where steam rose from thermal activity. He called the area Reykjavik, which means Smoky Bay.

In contrast with the protracted voyages, my flight from Glasgow to Iceland was quick and comfortable. The DC-8 climbed through layers of clouds of various shades and attained its cruising height of 31,000 ft in the sunlit air above.

Below the cloud were islands stretching like stepping stones from the north of Scotland towards Iceland. I recited the names as though in a litany—Orkney, Fair Isle, Shetland, the Faeroes: all part of Puffindom.

The Icelandair in-flight magazine urged me to buy Icelandic perfumes. On another page, a bottle of 'Monts Bleus' was set against a picture showing a peaty pool, bogland, angelica, a tobacco-brown plain and dark hills crusted with glacial ice.

I drew my holiday reading from a bag. This was *Iceland Spring*, by Dorothy Una Ratcliffe, published in 1949. She related how fortunate she was to secure a seat on the American flagship *Oslo*—a four-engined DC-4 Skymaster, which carried a crew of nine.

The *Oslo* flew north-westwards at 215 miles an hour, reaching an elevation of six thousand feet, passing over the Paps of Jura and tiny Iona; over Tiree and the Minch to the Outer Islands. 'We headed into a sundown of amber and orange-rose.' A strong headwind blew up after dark, so the Captain directed the aircraft to eight thousand feet and passed through several squalls, 'then for a while. . . over a Cloud Cuckoo-Land of Dark Blue cotton wool.'

After a comparatively brief flight, our big jet, its engines screaming, touched down on a runway which was laval brown. This was

Keflavik. We cruised to a terminal building which had something of the Nordic flavour in a roof supported by ribs, like those of an upturned longboat.

Strong beer (above 2.2%) being unavailable in Iceland, many of the returning Icelanders queued at the duty free shop in the airport to obtain a supply of stronger brands. 'Polar Beer' was a local brew. Icelandic Black Death, to use its unofficial name, is pure spirit with caraway seeds.

In Iceland, a land which runs hot and cold from the activity of volcano and glacier, the Norse gods had mixed a weather cocktail—sun, shower, rays of light, gloom, drizzle, rainbows, more drizzle and the brilliant stub-ends of yet more rainbows shimmering against dark clouds.

For the duration of my visit, there was no true darkness. At midnight, the sun tickled the horizon and then climbed once more. I encountered the Icelandic summer habit of calling on friends at midnight or when the limited television service closed down.

Ralph and Ella, at their home on the edge of Reykjavik, provided me with a meal featuring salmon, taken from the local river. Hours later, after much talk, we drove at midnight to the sea's edge for a view of a salmon-pink sky—and the distant form of Snaefell Glacier, some sixty miles away.

Another day, we toured a nearby village, consisting of historic houses which had been re-assembled here as evidence of Icelandic heritage. The houses were of wood, some with grassed-over roofs. Ella remembered when Grannie milked the cows in one of the complexes, where living quarters and farm buildings were under a succession of adjacent roofs.

I turned the conversation to the puffin and—knowing of the local partiality for puffin meat—asked how one might cook the bird. Ella telephoned a friend; they chatted for a while. Then I was told that only the puffin breast is eaten and that a minimum of four should be cooked at a time.

First remove the skin and take out the 'inners'; put the remainder in milk and water overnight, then wipe it down with a cloth and, using only the breast, as mentioned, coat in white flour, to which salt and pepper have been added.

Place equal parts of margarine and butter in a frying pan and brown the flesh. Then place it in boiling water, using sufficient to cover it. Bring the water to the boil and add cranberries, if it has not already been decided to eat puffin with cranberry jelly.

Boil for about half an hour, or until it is tender, when a little gravy browning should be added. Remove the puffin meat from the pot, keeping it warm in a dish. Put the gravy through a strainer and use water and season to taste, adding a little jelly and cream. Spread the gravy over the breast. It's simple, really!

In a book about life in Norway, I read that puffin-pie is 'not bad' if properly cooked. 'The backbone must be removed and the bird soaked in water for some hours before cooking or it will taste of fish.'

Ralph's excellent library included the book *Travels in the Island of Iceland,* by Sir George Stewart Mackenzie, published in 1811, which mentioned that Icelanders vigorously pursued sea birds for their eggs and feathers.

Sabine Baring-Gould, Anglican priest and writer, had a brief note about puffins in his book *Iceland: Its Scenes and Sagas* (1863), observing: 'At the beginning of October, the puffins betake themselves to the open sea, returning to their nesting quarters at the beginning of May.'

A lake near the heart of Reykjavik was the playground of terns. Their coarse voices—*keeyah, keeyah, keeyah*—seemed inappropriate to such fairylike creatures. Arctic terns leave Iceland with the waning year, flying far south until many birds are wintering among the ice-floes of Antarctica. First year birds may spend

their immaturity in circumnavigating the southern polar seas. Then they make the astonishing return journey to the edge of the Arctic to breed.

I mounted an expedition to locate an extinct member of the auk family—the great auk, or garefowl, a flightless species 'like a giant razorbill', which was last seen on an islet off Iceland in 1844. Might the evolutionary process lead to the Atlantic puffin becoming flightless?

A few inquiries at the bus station led me to the Natural History museum, where the collection includes a stuffed specimen of the lost auk and one of its eggs. The skin, which had been collected by a Danish nobleman, Count Raben, who visited Iceland in 1821, was auctioned by Sotheby's of London in 1971 and purchased for the Icelandic museum in America in 1975.

Presumably, the great auk—like the puffin—once had the ability to fly but the wings became increasingly used for propulsion in the sea, as have the flippers of the penguin, a bird of the southern ocean which has a name originally used for the great auk of northern waters. The great auk was 'penguin' to the old voyagers who, when they saw something akin to it in Antarctica, used the same name.

Not being able to fly, the great auk swam vast distances when on migration. Bones found in ancient middens indicate that it nested around the North Atlantic, with a particularly large concentration in Newfoundland.

Europeans, exploiting the rich fishing grounds, slew the docile auks for food, driving the luckless birds into pens and clubbing them to death. Richard Whitbourne, writing in 1620, noted it was 'as if God had made the innocency of so poore a creature to become such an admirable instrument for the sustentation of man.'

As each pair of auks produced one egg a year, there was no chance of the species perpetuating itself in the face of such slaughter. The auk became extinct in North America between 1800 and 1825. It had vanished from the Faeroes by about 1800, from Greenland by 1815 and from Britain (St Kilda) in 1821.

A few great auks remained on one of the bird-haunted skerries of the Westman Islands, and in particularly on Geirfuglasker, which tilted as though nature intended to give easy access to a flightless auk which was so large and ungainly on land.

Even here, the auk was not safe, though the approach was hazardous to fowlers, several of whom were drowned in rough conditions. The auks transferred their nesting place to the isle of Eldey. As the species became rare, egg-collectors scrambled for the last specimens.

Two birds were seen on Eldey in 1844. As men landed to catch them, the auks struggled to escape but were overtaken and slain. A single egg, found to be chipped, was tossed away.

Reykjavik:
Shopping for Puffins

THE MAIN centre of the Puffin world is Iceland, where the population is several times greater than that of all other countries combined.

M P Harris, 1984.

THE TOURIST will discover the incredible contrasts. . .grassy plains, low hills, fertile heathlands and stern mountains. And above the green mantle of the earth, white patches of snow glitter deep in between jet-black precipices and steep mountain peaks. . .There is an abundance of sea-birds everywhere along the coast and on the islands.

Brochure about Northern Iceland.

COLOUR ringing of very large numbers of Puffins in northern Britain has proved that some birds move to breed on the Isle of May from the Farne Islands further south, where increasing numbers have caused a shortage of space. Some birds have moved between colonies elsewhere, such as St Kilda and Great Saltee, southeast Ireland, and a few have gone north to Iceland and the Faeroe Islands from Britain.

Clare Lloyd, 1981.

PUFFIN appears to be a English word, later borrowed by the French, but it can only be traced back to the four-teenth century. Its origin, as Phillips suggests in 1706, is probably from puff, to puff out, 'a bird supposed to be so called from its round belly, as it were swelling or puffing out,' with the suffix denoting a diminutive.

C A Gibson-Hill, 1947.

IN THE shops of Reykjavik, images of the Atlantic puffin stared back at me from postcards and posters, from book jackets and tea towels. I saw puffins galore as I scanned the tourist literature in the main information centre.

A lady assistant was a Westman Islander—a native of Heimaey, a scattering of volcanic islands lying just off the south coast. From her I had a first-hand account of what happens when some puffin fledglings leave their nesting burrows for the sea. Attracted by the bright lights of the town, they wander into the streets and are rescued by children, who put them into large boxes overnight. Next day, the young puffins are released from one of the lava-black beaches on another stretch of coast.

A tourist leaflet about the Westman group mentioned the millions of 'feathered visitors. . . not forgetting the puffin, which is the unofficial emblem of the Islands'.

I continued my exploration of Reykjavik, taking a lift to the top of the tower of the main (concrete) church, from which I scanned a city consisting mainly of small detached houses of corrugated zinc, painted in rainbow hues to give a spectacularly colourful effect against the blues and greys of the bay and its flanking fells.

I had coffee and cake at the *Norse Hutte* and attended the *Volcano Show,* the owner of which had gone, literally hot-foot, to the volcanic zone around Lake Myvatn to await an expected eruption. At the docks, an immature glaucous gull had joined the lesser black-backed gulls rifling fish boxes on the back of a lorry.

Having heard that 'breast of puffin' was available, vacuum-packed, in the supermarkets of Reykjavik, I visited a store near the bus station. Many island communities of the North Atlantic had to live off the eggs and carcasses of seabirds. In Iceland, men performed stirring deeds while collecting eggs on the great cliffs of the Westfjords.

Puffin-catching is no longer on the old-time scale, but many puffins are slain, to be smoked or deep-frozen for later use. The dark meat does not taste unduly fishy. Centuries ago, when Lent was rigidly observed in the western world, the Church permitted puffin meat to be eaten in the week before Easter Day.

At the supermarket, I half expected to see frozen puffin exhibited in strips, like so many rashers of bacon, with a picture of a puffin and the name LUNDI boldly displayed on the label. The young man who attended to me vanished into a cold storage area and returned empty-handed. 'I think we have some lundi in the cellar.'

Puffin with chick in the nesting burrow.

Five minutes later, he was back with a plastic bag containing perhaps a score of lumps of dark flesh—puffin breast meat. He looked bemused, and rightly so, when I simply thanked him cordially and walked out of the store.

Of the many islands within sight of Reykjavik, there is but one which is patronised by puffins. Twenty of us, of various nationalities, put down our names to see Puffin Island. We were conveyed by motor cruiser. The greys of sea and sky merged. Mercifully, the water was calm.

It was not just a matter of seeing puffins; all good tourists must have pictorial proof. At the sight of the first puffin, a dozen cameras were brought into action.

The bird was afloat, with that look of surprise a puffin always seems to have, even when in repose. It swam away, looking back over its shoulder, as though expecting trouble. In the world of the Atlantic puffin, this is a reasonable supposition. Its enemies are numerous. I heard a whirr of camera shutters as other puffins appeared. Soon the air was buzzing with birds.

The island was small and appeared to be tilting. The shoreline consisted of jumbled boulders, though away from the sea lay soil and grass. Puffins stood like rows of skittles about their nesting holes.

I stayed for a few days at Hella, which is unusual in an Icelandic context, being a settlement lying away from the coast. This huddle of buildings developed around a shop which was constructed as recently as 1927, and Hella soon became a centre for trade, industry and tourism.

I do not recommend Iceland for sufferers from agoraphobia. So flat is the terrain and so clear the air that a range of mountains which appears close at hand might be forty miles away. One day, I set off to walk along a dusty road to a handy farm. After two hours of walking, that farm seemed no nearer than when I began

For several days, I spent most of my bird-watching time in an anorak. There was incessant rain, creating puddles which, when traffic-stirred, were yellow. Cars with headlamps glowing moved along the laval roads, trailing skirts of yellow spray. A drove of Icelandic ponies was yellow up to the hocks from wet mud.

An ornithological highlight was a black-tailed godwit in its breeding plumage. The bright chestnut of the head, neck and breast, stood out against the lush green of an Icelandic meadow.

A bus took me eastwards across a lava desert to the Promised Land—a valley leading up to a glacier. Red-necked phalarope spun on pools to stir up insect life, which the birds picked up with bills that looked as fine as needles.

Gannets.

Thence to the settlement of Vik—one of many Viks throughout the Norse world, this being the name for a creek. The Icelandic Vik once had a harbour, but land disturbances caused the sea to retreat and by the 1920s the harbour was unusable. I scanned a hill overlooking Vik. On the seaward side, now a kilometre away from salt water, is a vast nesting colony of puffins. When returning to their burrows with food, the birds run the gauntlet—over water as well as land—of kleptoparasitic Arctic skuas.

Two students of puffins, Arnason and Grant, discovered that the puffins of Vik are most vulnerable to predation by the skua, this 'pirate' of the airlanes. Studying the food brought by the puffins, the two scientists concluded that about 4% of all incoming loads of fish-food for the young were dropped, 1.7% were eaten by skuas and 1% fell to the ground and were eaten by gulls. A figure of 1.2% represented food lost in the vegetation.

Not wishing to add further to the problems of this South Coast colony, which has to do its best in trying circumstances, I followed a byroad to the black beach (near which I disturbed a cock ptarmigan). Two prominent rock stacks were pointed out as 'troll-women'. They went wading into the sea to fish and began gossiping. When the sun came up, and they had not regained their subterranean home, they were turned into stone.

A light mist clung to the coast. A few gannets, doubtless from the colony on Eldey, were in passage. Puffins swarmed like bees. Puffins stared down from near their nesting burrows.

With a precipitation of 2,300 mm a year, Vik is one of the wettest places in Iceland. The seabirds have extra need of oil glands to waterproof their feathers. So have the Arctic terns. Extending across low ground, on either side of the road, was a huge ternery. Any humans who tested the defences retired with bruised heads, caused by jabs from the beaks of the birds—beaks which (appropriately) are coloured red.

Westman Islands:

By Air to Heimaey

SEVERAL of us rushed through the evening meal—the cauliflower soup, boiled lamb chops, mixed salad, potatoes and carrots. We had booked a flight from the grassed-over runway at Hella to Heimaey, the largest of the Westman Islands.

A twin-engined aircraft arrived from Reykjavik and we were soon aloft, enjoying the spectacle of a vast, flat plain, with a gleam from river and irrigation ditches. Inland was Hekla and its retinue of high fells, daubed with snow.

Fifteen islands and innumerable stacks and skerries compose the Westman group, which was thrust out of the sea by volcanic disturbance. A few Norse settlers, huddling on these rocks in the eighth century, could not have foreseen that as a base for fishing Heimaey would grow over the centuries into a large and resourceful community.

We circled in a gold-tinted sky, looking down on Helgafell (Holy Fell), an extinct volcano, and upon a heap of black ash which was all that remained of a volcano which erupted on January 23, 1973, leading to the temporary evacuation of the population. Buildings were destroyed and the environment re-modelled, but there was not a single human casualty.

For over four months, Heimaey spouted flame and smoke. A lava flow spread across half the town and covered the rest of the buildings with ash. Television film showed sea water in vast quantities being pumped on to the hot lava to halt its progress before it could block the harbour. The technique was successful.

So much we recalled as our aircraft banked. Into view came fish-drying racks, now little used. Touchdown was on a runway of fine cinders. We walked to the terminal building. Hanging from the main roof was an old-type aircraft.

The first bird to greet me to the Westmans was a golden plover, calling from the hill. A stuffed puffin above the dashboard of the small bus which was to take us for a tour of the island looked so lifelike I am sure it winked at me.

The driver told us the volcano had been a godsend, providing ash for the aircraft runway and some new roads. Part of the volcano had been set aside and a course marked with white-painted tyres let into the ground. It was now used by the motor bike-mad youth, who had previously been a nuisance in town.

Volcanic material was suitable aggregate for new building schemes. Heat from the volcano was piped for use domestically and, with volcanic lava narrowing but not closing the harbour, this facility had been much improved. Boats within the harbour had extra protection from gales.

Such had been the novelty of the flight and a downward glance at a town of 5,000 people set on a lump of rock rising from the North Atlantic, it did not seem incongruous, ten minutes later, to be in a bus being driven across a steaming volcano, which was taking on a reddish hue as the sun quested for the horizon. This day was already far spent but the light remained good.

Mosses and other plants had colonised parts of the lava field. It was suggested that the high rainfall had leached out noxious substances, allowing plants to grow and keeping them well watered.

From my brief association with Westman Islanders, I deduced they have drawn much of their outlook on life from their isolation. These are a tough, resourceful people, realistic in their outlook, hospitable by nature—and with a sense of fun. It was on Heimaey that the coach driver said: 'We catch fish. We eat fish. We talk about fish. We sell fish.' He paused, pointed to a group of three men and added: 'We look like fish'.

I asked the coach driver for the loan of his stuffed puffin. He readily agreed and smiled wrily as I positioned it in a cindery setting, photographing it at close range. The Westman Islanders eat the puffin. 'Salt it a little; it is quite good,' said the driver. Passengers on the ferry Herjolfur who patronise a cafeteria where hot meals are served, may select the Westman Islands delicacy of smoked puffin.

The Icelanders have long been conservation-minded and ships are forbidden to use steam-whistles or sirens unnecessarily near bird-cliffs, which was a regular occurrence last century so that visitors could marvel at the spectacle of a sky half full of whirling birds.

A prime nesting area is the 850 feet headland of Heimaklettur (Home Rock). It is a green-topped headland, and the rock holds many ledges—potential nesting sites for seabirds. The restless sea has gouged out many caves.

In the old days, and especially in the decade between 1850 and 1860, the puffins were trapped in nets placed over their burrows but the breeding stock declined so rapidly this practice was forbidden.

A hand-net called a *hafar* came into use, dead puffins being set up at the edge of the cliffs as decoys. A skilled fowler, intercepting puffins in their headlong flight, might account for up to a thousand birds in a day. Hand-netting is known as *fleyging,* being mostly practised in July and August. Over 150,000 birds a year are taken.

The writer of the tourist leaflet referred to another birding technique, known as *sprang,* which is the art of swinging by a rope across a cliff face. 'Visitors can try for themselves this unique test of agility...at a 'safe' site called Sprangan.'

104

Puffin with fish food for its young.

Our tour over, we flew from the dull red runway. As the aircraft climbed, it banked and the clustering Westman Islands could be taken in at a glance. We stared with awe at the new volcano, now so benign, so useful.

The pilot set course for Hella. Off the port side of the aircraft was the pink and gold of the low-lying sun. Off the starboard side lay an etheral blueness, with ranges of snow-crusted mountains, ice sheets and glaciers, flecked by shadow.

There was time, on my return, for a walk to the river and back. Shortly before midnight, the sun broke clear of cloud. Fierce rays swept the area. Some of the windows of Hella caught the eye of the sun and appeared to be plated with gold.

Northern Iceland:
Fast Boat to Puffin Island

A FOKKER Friendship twin-engined aircraft was my transport to
the north coast of Iceland. The pilot circled Reykjavik, and I settled beside a window of the aircraft and cocked the shutter of my
cameras in the expectation of glorious aerial views of the Interior.
I saw—cloud.

An occasional gap revealed hills which had patches of snow in
their ancient joints. But mainly we flew at 13,000 feet in a sunless
world. The aircraft was swaddled in cloud. A diversion came when
we were provided with hot drinks.

In due course, the Fokker rolled to a halt beside a terminal
building set in a 2,000 year-old lavascape. In the absence of direc-
tional light, the scene was dreary. Even the trees seemed to have
lost heart and stopped growing. I mentioned their modest size to
a local man. He replied: 'In Iceland, anything that grows above one
metre is called a tree...'

The man who drove the bus from the airport to Husavik had
strong Nordic features—lean face, blonde hair—but he was actual-
ly a Dutchman, not a descendant of the Swedish Viking, Gardar
Svarvarsson, who named the north-coast settlement, now a fishing
town, after 'bay of houses'.

The bus driver had married an Icelander and settled here. We
crossed the Laxa river, named after the Norse word for salmon.
It is also a resort of the Harlequin duck. The drake looks like a
fragment of a rainbow fallen into the water. The charge for angling
was about £500 for a half day. A man who caught nothing

lamented that he had not even had the bad-luck of hooking and losing a twenty-pounder.

So we came to Husavik (pronounced Oosavik), on a bay of Skjalfandi, overlooking the Arctic Ocean. The small trading station of half a century ago had burgeoned into a town with a good range of services, while still being dominated by its green and white wooden church, which has a cloud-tickling spire.

My bedroom window overlooked Husavikurfjall, a haunt of golden plover. Hot water which gushed from the hotel's taps came from thermal sources and carried with it the tang of sulphur. In the capacious dining room, I was served with mushroom soup with peppers; rainbow trout with shrimp sauce; carrots, courgettes and side salad; pineapple mousee with cream and cherry; followed by coffee.

Mist and rain persisted for a day or two. Cars with blazing headlamps splashed through yellow puddles in the laval grit and, themselves, took on the pervading yellow hue. A glance over the harbour wall revealed a misty sea, as calm and uninteresting as water in a bath-tub—until I noticed scores of fulmar petrels, attracted by the outflow of a fish factory, paddling silently on the water and periodically bending their thick necks to collect morsels.

The weather changed suddenly, like a transformation scene at a pantomime. All was revealed with clarity and colour.

After an evening meal of roast lamb and roast potatoes, followed by fruit pie and cream, I voyaged to Puffin Island. The boat-owner led the way along a jetty against which boats seemed to have been moored in order of size, the largest first. Our craft, towards the end of the line, was a small, fibre-glass boat with a deck house forrard.

I expected the boat to chug out of harbour with a rattling engine and exhaust fumes clouding the still air, but this craft had a

155 hp engine. The proud owner, with a wry smile, opened her up even before we had left the harbour. Up went the bows and, from the stern, the wake rose and spread like jets of water on an ornamental fountain.

Husavik declined rapidly. My eye was fixed on the most attractive feature, the wooden church, but soon we were on the Arctic Ocean with sheets of silver spray obscuring a view of a cliffbound stretch of the north coast.

Birds buzzed around Puffin Island. The sea was speckled with their plump, two-tone bodies. The boat overtook a few birds, one with fish in its mandibles. It took off, despairingly, breasting the water, working its wings and webbed feet until there was sufficient power for flight.

The sea was turquoise blue, capturing the blueness of the sky. The island was clearly delineated by a sun which burned in the sky like a celestial blow-lamp. I had entertained a faint hope we would

Cormorants at their nesting islet.

Young puffins.

land on Puffin Island, but it was like a medieval moated castle with high walls and the drawbridge raised.

Two naturalists who had arrived in a large boat had been put ashore in a dinghy and were now climbing a fissured area using ropes. The tackle they carried included long-handled puffin nets. They would stay in a small hut where presumably they were studying puffins, for it was too early for the annual cull of birds to take place.

We circled round the island, seeing a navigation light and the remains of a wooden winch which had been used for hauling boats up the cliff. The winch assembly was in two sections—a frame to hold the winding device, which would be hand-operated, and a lower structure, with wooden rollers, positioned so that whatever was being raised did not brush against the lower cliff.

Above the main cliffs, Puffin Island was banded, there being alternate layers of rock and grass. The grassy areas were presumably where the puffins had drilled their nesting burrows.

I felt sorry for the puffins, which were having fish filched from them by other bird species, notably the Arctic skua, which slid through the air like a sea-hawk, two elongated central tail feathers aiding its ability to manoevre rapidly as it prepared to outfly a puffin.

The skua accelerated and, like a programmed missile, it 'locked' itself on to the course of a fish-carrying bird, which was not close enough to the colony to be able to reach its nesting burrow without being robbed. The puffin had the disadvantage of being followed slightly to one side, where it could not keep its pursuer in view.

The skua's dash was short and sharp. The two birds descended until, a few yards above the sea, the puffin simply stopped beating its wings and plopped into the water. A jet of water marked the point of entry. Normally, a skua attempts to persuade the puffin to drop its prey in mid-air, allowing time to collect the fish before it reaches the sea. Such a strong predator as a skua may even jostle the bird.

A puffin which ran the gauntlet of the skuas was robbed by a gull as it touched down near its burrow. Sometimes puffins circle until several birds are in the air and they descend together, confusing the hostile reception party.

The puffin slopes were speckled with other gulls, which presumably were waiting for a puffin to land with a load of fish which might be wrested from it.

It was pleasant to sit on the gunwhale of the boat. The lowering sun gave a pinkish hue to Puffin Island as it diminished in size during the homeward voyage. Now we saw only its shady side—a purple block against the sea-tones and the spouting wake of the boat.

The fulmar petrels which approached from the stern and glided low over our heads had a pinkish tinge.

Grimsey:
A Speck in the Ocean

NETS may not be used for bird-hunting on land. It shall, however, be permitted to catch Puffins by net in places where their burrowing activity interferes with Eider-duck breeding.

From an Icelandic bird protection Act, 1966.

THE (puffin) colonies on Grimsey in the north are large and the birds nest in grassy slopes and boulders, not only high up the slopes as in Britain, but at sea level.

M P Harris, 1984.

AT DAWN, the sea surrounding the islands where puffins breed numerously will be dotted with young puffins which have made their way to the water during the night. They have scrambled over rocks or fluttered down from high cliffs. The strong tides will help to sweep them away to sea. The young bird paddles vigorously (for as yet it cannot fly), showing anxiety to get out into the open ocean.

James Fisher.

MY ACCOMMODATION at Akureyri had the grand title of *Hotel Edda*. The evening meal was served in a pillared hall. Five of us left before the pudding was served. We had booked a passage on the evening flight to Grimsey, an island which, though little more than a speck on the map, is famous. It is bisected by the Arctic Circle.

The airport official took special pains when announcing the flight: he repeated the name 'Grimsey Island' several times and stated that the aircraft was 'that little yellow and orange plane on the far side of the tarmac'. It turned out to be a Canadian-built de Havilland Twin Otter, with two engines, each generating 660 horse-power.

The seats had been re-arranged to leave space for the mail, which was protected by a padlocked waterproof bag. I joined a young couple from East Anglia, a lad from London, two hulking Americans, a girl returning to her island home, a taciturn ornithologist—and a Welsh opera singer.

We went through the normal pre-flight safety routine, donned our seat belts and noted from a sign behind every seat: 'Life Vest Under Your Seat—for your Comfort'. Hmmm. The pilot announced we would reach Grimsey in twenty-five minutes.

Two engines reached the right degree of power and with a roar we raced down the runway and took to the air. Ducks at the edge of the river, not far from the runway, unconcernedly went about the business of feeding.

It was 8-30 p.m., with plenty of daylight left. The aircraft droned over Eyjafjordur, a fan-like cut into the much indented north coast of Iceland. Cloud and drizzle blunted details of the landscape. We flew in a murky world, with the sea as dull-looking as used bathwater.

After an uneventful trip and a view beneath of grey sea, we descended to Grimsey, seeing a natural rock arch, fish-drying racks, a small village grouped round a harbour—and the runway. We passed between two halves of a massive Arctic tern colony. The birds were ferocious, having chicks at a feathered stage. Some were even trying their wings and undertaking short flights.

A rusty tractor with a scoop attachment was driven towards the plane. For one moment, the Welsh opera singer entertained the thought that we must step into the scoop and be lowered to the ground. It was, in fact, to collect the goods being delivered by our plane.

The terminal building, of modest size, had the name 'Grimsey' above it in prominent letters. Inside, the place was a scene rather like an 'ops' room in a wartime film. The fields beyond were spangled with yellow flowers. Spring is tardy on this tiny lump of an island on the Arctic Circle.

I made directly to a post indicating the imaginary line which girdles the northern hemisphere. A sign informed me I was 1,972 km from London.

The terns wheeled, dived and pecked. It amused me to see young terns trying out 'circuits and bumps' on the runway. One flightless tern, which had snuggled against a tuft of grass, had a bill of deep red beak and a body fuzzy with the down of infancy.

Rain was hurled at me by a wind full of spite. I quested for the west coast with all the determination of a pufling on its first journey. Suddenly, I was at the rim of Grimsey, here a line of low cliffs. There was a fringe of puffins.

It surprised me that they were virtually at sea level, lining the tops of the cliffs, their burrows in the soil just below the turf. These Grimsey puffins were true northerners, *Fratercula arctica arctica,* and noticeably larger than those I had seen in Britain. They also seemed more nervous, quicker to take flight. I approached one group by dint of moving on all fours, and keeping out of sight.

A puffin which took off from the sea had to compromise between swimming and flying. It took to the air with much effort, its wings vibrating like tuning forks—some half dozen times a second—and the webbed feet paddling until there was enough lift to get the bird airborne.

In a few weeks, with the nesting season over, the puffins would be far out to sea, moulting into a drab winter garb. The outer sheaths of the bill would peel away; the face would darken and the ornaments around the eye would vanish.

On Grimsey, which that day lived up to its name, rain and cloud swept by, making photography chancy. I walked along the clifftop. Eiders and their young bobbed like feathered corks on the ocean swell. There was no time before the return flight to walk around the island.

I strode along the runway, beside which was a shallow ridge of cast tern feathers. Adult birds rose, circled and jerked their way across the sky, uttering their creaky calls. The young birds flew with what I took to be grave deliberation. Their wings looked blunt at the tips.

Only two corpses appeared among the litter of weed and feathers. The terns of Grimsey appeared to recognise the lethal potential of the aircraft. Redshank and snipe contributed to the medley of sound on this semi-Arctic island.

The pilot welcomed us aboard his aircraft and warmed up the engines. At 10 p.m., we left the runway and as the aircraft banked the small fishing village returned to view.

The Welsh opera singer, looking into the murk, and at the water dribbling from a wing strut of the aircraft, said: 'If this is high summer, God help them in winter!'

We crossed the coast. Sea-greys merged gently with sky-grey. When the mainland was visible, it was just a grey smudge. The opera singer, autographing my notebook, used gentle irony: 'To Bill. Had a marvellous time up in the snows of the Arctic'.

Soon we were circling over Akureyri's neat pattern of streets and homes, with a multi-tinted collection of roofs. At the airport, I was handed a *Certificate of Achievement,* testifying that I had 'reached the Arctic Region by air and crossed the Arctic Circle on land at the Island of Grimsey off the north coast of Iceland at 66 deg 33″ N, 18 deg 01″ W'.

* * *

The aircraft conveying me back to Britain took off precisely on time and soared through a grey mist to attain the blue regions beyond. Away from land, the mist and cloud fell away. Now there was a general blueness—that of space—and below was a deep blue ocean.

The breakfast was appetising. The inclination to 'nod off' proved strong. I dreamed about glaciers, about lava and thundering waterfalls, about ponies and, of course, about puffins, soon to disperse across the North Atlantic.

The young puffin, if adequately fed by its parents, becomes a podgy bird. Its glossy new plumage is still obscured by fluffy down, which then is moulted, the tufts joining the litter on the floor of the burrow.

It is an astonishing transformation. The bird, receiving less food for several days, slims down to its operational weight. The parents' work is done.

On a moonless night, when the predator gulls are roosting, the pufling makes its break for freedom. It will have nothing to do with its parents again. A bird which for weeks has known the security of a dry chamber scurries towards the sea on legs which have been strengthened by its subterranean exercises.

Some youngsters are trapped among rocks; others walk into blind alleys but an appreciable number live to reach the sea and are soon using their feet as paddles. The wild sea is about them. They are as buoyant as corks as they strike out for—who knows where?

A young puffin—with no parental supervision—can dive, feed and ultimately fly. It is on its own, a mere speck on the grey wastes of the North Atlantic.

It will not set foot on land again for two or three years.

I opened my eyes, after my dream sequence, to find that Scotland was below me, clear of cloud and in all the lushness of its summer green. We descended towards Glasgow airport, with Arran's splendid peaks rising above a cushion of vapour.

The Icelandair plane touched down and trundled towards the terminal. There was not a puffin in sight.

DAVID BINNS.

"Castleberg" Books
by W R Mitchell

Stocks Re-visited

Life in Upper Hodder Valley before Stocks Reservoir was constructed to supply the Fylde. Based on taped interviews with former residents. Photographs and line drawings. 120 pages.

ISBN: 1 871064 96 1   £5.60

The Lost Village of Mardale (Haweswater)

Tales from the Lakeland valley before and during the creation of a reservoir to supply Manchester. Photographs and drawings. 120 pages.

ISBN: 1 871064 92 9   £5.99

The Men who Made the Settle-Carlisle

Edited version of three former "Castleberg" titles—about Shanty Life, How they Built the fell-top railway and Footplate Tales. 120 pages.

ISBN: 1 871064 86 4   £5.99

Hotfoot to Haworth

The absorbing story of pilgrimage to the shrine of the Bronte family, from the arrival of the Duke of Devonshire with a brace of grouse to the mass invasion of today. 96 pages.

ISBN: 1 871064 75 9   £4.99

Lakeland Laughter

In conjunction with Radio Cumbria and including humorous tales sent in by listeners. Drawings by Ionicus. 120 pages.

ISBN: 1 871064 91 0   £5.40

Yorkshire Laughter

Native Wit and Humour. Foreword by Freddie Trueman, OBE. Cover and drawings by Ionicus. 96 pages.

ISBN: 1 871064 85 6   £4.99

Drystone Walls of the Yorkshire Dales

Taped interviews with drystone wallers and historical background to walls. Folklore and natural history. Foreword by Richard Muir. 96 pages.

ISBN: 1 871064 80 5   £5.20

Mr Elgar and Dr Buck

A fifty year long friendship between the famous composer and a Dales doctor. Many illustrations, including facsimile pages from Elgarian letters. Foreword by Lady Barbirolli. 122 pages.

ISBN: 1 871064 05 8   £5.60

✳   ✳   ✳

Book list from "Castleberg", 18 Yealand Avenue, Giggleswick, Settle, North Yorkshire, BD24 0AY.